# THE KRAYS' LONDON

*For my Uncle, Paul King, who would have loved to have read this book.*

# THE KRAYS' LONDON
## A HISTORY AND GUIDE

**CAROLINE ALLEN**

PEN & SWORD HISTORY
AN IMPRINT OF PEN & SWORD BOOKS LTD.
YORKSHIRE – PHILADELPHIA

First published in Great Britain in 2019 by
**PEN AND SWORD HISTORY**
*an imprint of*
Pen & Sword Books Ltd
Yorkshire – Philadelphia

Copyright © Caroline Allen, 2019

ISBN 978 1 52673 381 8

The right of Caroline Allen to be identified
as Author of this work has been asserted by her in accordance
with the Copyright, Designs and Patents Act 1988.

A CIP catalogue record for this book is available from the British Library.
All rights reserved. No part of this book may be reproduced or
transmitted in any form or by any means, electronic or
mechanical including photocopying, recording or
by any information storage and retrieval system, without
permission from the Publisher in writing.

Printed and bound in India by Replika Press Pvt. Ltd.

Typeset in Times New Roman 11/13 by
Aura Technology and Software Services, India

Pen & Sword Books Ltd incorporates the Imprints of Pen & Sword Books
Archaeology, Atlas, Aviation, Battleground, Discovery,
Family History, History, Maritime, Military, Naval, Politics, Railways,
Select, Transport, True Crime, Fiction, Frontline Books, Leo Cooper,
Praetorian Press, Seaforth Publishing, Wharncliffe and White Owl.

For a complete list of Pen & Sword titles please contact
**PEN & SWORD BOOKS LIMITED**
47 Church Street, Barnsley, South Yorkshire, S70 2AS, England
E-mail: enquiries@pen-and-sword.co.uk
Website: www.pen-and-sword.co.uk

Or

**PEN AND SWORD BOOKS**
1950 Lawrence Rd, Havertown, PA 19083, USA
E-mail: Uspen-and-sword@casematepublishers.com
Website: www.penandswordbooks.com

# Contents

| | | |
|---|---|---|
| Introduction | | 8 |
| Chapter 1 | 178 Vallance Road | 12 |
| Chapter 2 | Wood Close School | 20 |
| Chapter 3 | Daniel Street School | 24 |
| Chapter 4 | Repton Boxing Club | 27 |
| Chapter 5 | G. Kelly Pie & Mash | 35 |
| Chapter 6 | The Regal | 39 |
| Chapter 7 | Chris' Hairdressers | 44 |
| Chapter 8 | The Double R Club | 48 |
| Chapter 9 | E. Pellicci's Cafe | 52 |
| Chapter 10 | 57 Ormsby Street | 56 |
| Chapter 11 | The Kentucky | 59 |
| Chapter 12 | Wandsworth Prison | 63 |
| Chapter 13 | Esmeralda's Barn | 66 |
| Chapter 14 | The Hideaway/El Morocco | 70 |
| Chapter 15 | St James The Great Church | 74 |
| Chapter 16 | Cedra Court | 77 |
| Chapter 17 | 34 Wimborne Court | 81 |
| Chapter 18 | The Lion | 84 |
| Chapter 19 | The Blind Beggar | 87 |
| Chapter 20 | 206a Barking Road | 92 |
| Chapter 21 | The Regency | 96 |
| Chapter 22 | The Carpenter's Arms | 99 |
| Chapter 23 | 97 Evering Road | 102 |
| Chapter 24 | Grave Maurice | 105 |
| Chapter 25 | The Old Horns | 108 |

| Chapter 26 | Braithwaite House | 111 |
| Chapter 27 | HM Brixton Prison | 114 |
| Chapter 28 | Old Street Magistrates' Court | 116 |
| Chapter 29 | The Old Bailey | 118 |
| Chapter 30 | All Saints Church | 121 |
| Chapter 31 | St Matthew's Church | 123 |
| Chapter 32 | W. English & Son | 128 |
| Chapter 33 | Chingford Mount Cemetery | 131 |
| Sources | | 133 |

Photography by James Allen

# A GUIDE TO THE
# KRAYS' LONDON

# Introduction

There are many conflicting stories about who Ronnie and Reggie Kray were. Films depicting their lives have made the public vilify, adore and even admire the East End gangsters.

The pair were standout perpetrators of organised crime in the 1950s and '60s, and most people who lived in the East End of London during that time have a story or two to share about them.

Before I delve into the frequented haunts of the Kray twins, it's important to share a bit of information about what the East End was like during the years of their reign. I believe this to be quite an important part of their story.

This area of London was poor. This is a sentence that has been repeated time and time again during the interview process for this book. It was overcrowded and with overcrowding came a whole plethora of social problems. The poverty dates back to the beginning of the nineteenth century when the East End's land operated on a system called copyhold, which – in simple terms – meant that the land was held on short leases, stopping people from developing on it.

The Second World War had a devastating impact on the East End of London. Born in 1933, the Kray twins were just children during the war, but the area in which they were born was badly battered.

When the war was over, the proximity to the docks, which attracted immigration and low-paid, manual workers, was perhaps the most prominent reason why this area was overcrowded in such a disproportionate way to the rest of London.

The East End was a prime location for industries producing noxious gases. The location of this part of London was key. Winds travelled from west to east in the city so by placing factories in the East End, the gases would travel away from the city and not into it. This meant there was always a lot of jobs for working-class people.

At the time, the people of Bethnal Green, Poplar and Stepney were no strangers to crime. Theft of goods at the quayside and prostitution were rife during the years before the Krays were born. The area also had a history of attracting notorious criminals, from Jack The Ripper to the London Burkers.

Throughout all of this, East Enders formed an alliance. They weren't despondent about their lot in life, instead, they were largely a happy and friendly community. I've spoken to a number of people who would refer to themselves as 'cockneys' (to be a cockney you must have been born within earshot of the Bow bells), and their memories of the East End during the 1950s and '60s are overwhelmingly positive.

*Introduction*

*A building close by to the school the twins attended. Taken in 2018.*

In those years, being poor didn't mean you didn't enjoy life. All of the people I interviewed said that East End people were very proud of their houses and they'd always be spotlessly clean, happy and largely content.

In a community as tight-knit as this, you can see why people defended the twins. Many of the people in roads around Vallance Road, where the pair grew up, knew their mother, Violet. This integrated community, coupled with the area's deep mistrust of the police, caused a wave of support for them.

It's important to remember that during this time, the Kray twins were very much a part of everyday activity for a typical cockney. They might pass them in the street and say hello. The population of the East End felt mostly safe from the Kray twins, because they were 'their own'. Here was born a 'Robin Hood' mentality; people believed they only stole from, and murdered, people who deserved it and that they were doing it in the best interest of the people of the East End.

It can be argued that the Krays used this community camaraderie to their advantage. The pair used to take protection money from local shops and businesses. For example, if somebody vandalised their shop, owed them money or stole from them, the perpetrator would have the Krays to answer to.

This isn't the first time in history that we've seen criminals adored by the public. Take drug lord and narco-terrorist Pablo Escobar as an example. The people in Medellín, Colombia, worshipped him throughout the 1970s. Again, Medellín's poverty-stricken environment and mistrust of police led them to think Escobar was working on their behalf: the people's criminal.

*Bethnal Green Road, 2018.*

*A quiet road off Bethnal Green Road.*

*Introduction*

You can, as a result, forgive the many books and films which depict the Krays in a romantic way because it is, in fact, factually accurate of the way in which the people of the East End felt at the time.

This guidebook will take you, place by place, around where Ronnie and Reggie Kray lived and worked. Some of the places mentioned are still standing today and most of the roads are still there. The idea is not for me to either vilify or romanticise the duo; I think it's important everybody makes up their own minds. Instead, this book will take an in-depth look at what happened in each place and how their story pieced together to create such an iconic path.

# Chapter 1

# 178 Vallance Road

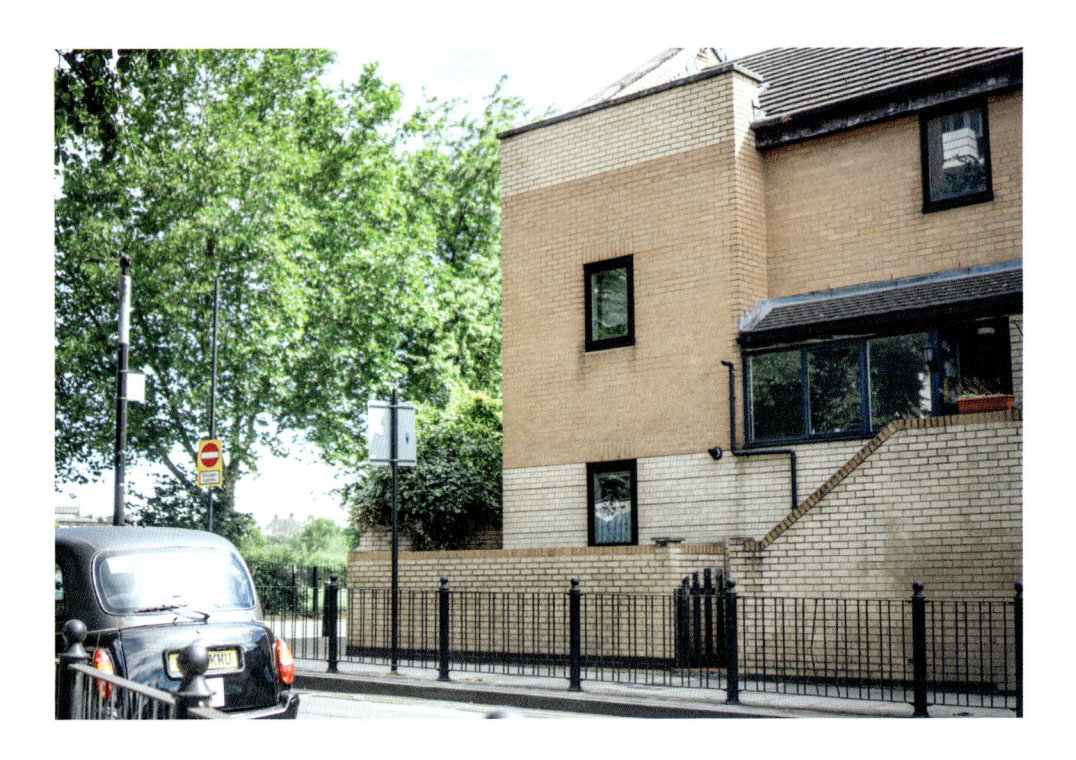

**Where?**
178 Vallance Road
Bethnal Green
London
E2 6HR

**Why?**
Other than jail, this Bethnal Green house was where the Kray twins lived most of their lives.

**How to get there:**
Bethnal Green Station is the nearest overground station to Vallance Road. From there, walk along the B135 towards Shoreditch. At the crossroads, go right onto

## 178 Vallance Road

Vallance Road; 178 Vallance Road is just off of the crossroads. The original building is no longer standing, but there are houses in its place. The original building was knocked down as part of the post-war East-End rejuvenation.

Many people think 178 Vallance Road – or Fort Vallance, as it was named – was where the Kray twins were born. In fact, they moved from Hoxton's Stean Street when they were aged 6. Reggie Kray was born at eight o'clock at night on 24 October 1933 – his Brother, Ron, was born ten minutes later.

Reggie has, on numerous occasions, described his first house in Stean Street as a 'depressing area of grey streets'. In their book *Our Story*, Reggie said: 'Some of the poorest houses and people in England were to be found there, my family were among them.'

The road, which can be found off of Queensbridge Road, is still fairly nondescript. The roads surrounding it are home to a mixture of older flats intertwined with new-builds and restaurants. Hoxton itself has seen something of a rejuvenation in recent years, following the likes of Shoreditch. It's now a regular drinking spot for young Londoners with an assortment of eateries and bars.

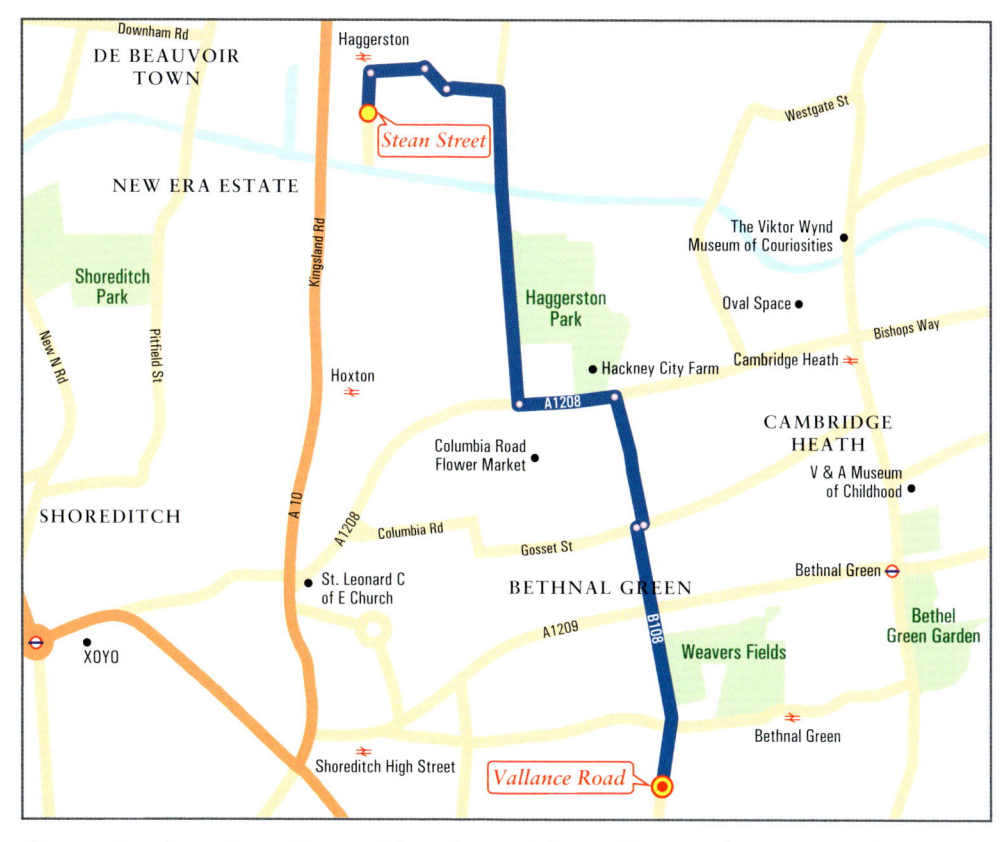

*Distance from Stean Street, Hoxton, (where Ronnie & Reggie Kray were born) to 178 Vallance Road, Bethnal Green, where they grew up.*

That wasn't always the way, though. Ronnie and Reggie lived in Stean Street with their mother, Violet, dad, Charles and older brother, Charles. Both their dad and older brother were known as Charlie. Violet was unhappy there, and the Krays eventually moved a mile and a half away to Vallance Road in Bethnal Green to be nearer to Violet's parents. A mile or so away from your parents hardly seems very far nowadays, but this really highlights the closeness and community of the East End lifestyle. In those days, Bethnal Green was also seen as a slightly better class of place to live than Hoxton.

As well as Violet's parents, the boys' Auntie Rose lived just around the corner from Vallance Road. The pair spoke fondly of their relationship with her and many people remarked that she was the opposite of Violet in many ways, commenting on how much harder and tougher she was than her sister.

I'll paint a picture of 178 Vallance Road for you. It's no longer standing, although there are houses in its place and the layout of the road is similar. It was a small, terraced house off Bethnal Green Road. Bethnal Green Road was – and still is – a key road which joins Bethnal Green to Shoreditch and then on to the rest of the City.

The house was the second in a terrace of four. There was no bathroom – which wasn't uncommon of houses in this area at this time. Instead, the lavatory was outside in the tiny back garden.

Liverpool Street Station is one of the busiest stations ferrying people in and out of London. Back then, it was just the same. The train lines out of Liverpool Street passed the end of 178 Vallance Road's garden all day and all night. People who had been there, or around the area, said the noise was deafening and non-stop.

# *178 Vallance Road*

There were no fields, nor even a patch of grass; even the trees looked like they had seen better days. But there were plenty of pubs. Every person I interviewed said the pubs were always brimming with people.

The Second World War started in 1939, when the Kray twins were almost 7. Anybody with a vague knowledge of the Second World War will know just how hard the East End, particularly Bethnal Green, was hit. This area contained some of the most important docklands and was a hub for imports and exports. The Germans believed that if they could disable the East End, they would cut off London's supplies. By 1940, the Germans referred to the East End as 'Target Area A'.

By the end of the war, 10,000 homes in Bethnal Green alone were destroyed. It's estimated that 47,000 homes in the East End were destroyed and 2,000 people killed.

People were evacuated out of Bethnal Green in their droves and it wasn't long after the Kray family settled in Vallance Road that they were told to leave. Families were ripped apart during this time. Many of the women in the East End were required to stay because of the importance of their jobs in the factories and warehouses, which meant many of the children were separated from their mothers at a young age.

The scene wasn't a pleasant one. A local resident talks of how she was shipped out of Bethnal Green within a matter of days. Aged 6, she lived just off of Vallance Road on nearby Chester Street:

> We were directed to leave, but Mum was staying behind. I was told my Aunt would be looking after us and we had to get on a train to meet her.

> At six, I didn't really understand what the war was or why I was being forced to move to a place I'd never been to before. I packed a small bag, with the help of my Mum, who was understandably stressed, and went to the station. What strikes me – as I've got older – is just how vague all of the instructions were. We were told to wait under a clock at the station, which wasn't uncommon, and our Aunt would pick us up.
>
> I remember Mum crying at the train station as I and hundreds of other children and women looked on through the windows. The following week she took a day off of her warehouse job and came to visit us. That evening her warehouse was bombed and everybody in it was killed. We're so, so thankful she came to visit us – she ended up living to be 88.

This story and hundreds of others like it go some way to highlight the importance of the evacuation. The whole process happened quickly and the families of the East End – and much of London – weren't afforded any time to pack properly and to say their goodbyes. The Kray family were no exception.

They were initially evacuated to a farm in Hadleigh, Suffolk, but Violet missed the East End and so they returned quite quickly. This was a bold move by their mother. Evacuation was voluntary, but much of the infrastructure of London was shut down. Many urban schools were closed and families were urged to send their children away to go to school in the countryside. A number of local adults were called upon to become volunteer marshals and ease the transition process for the younger population. In total, 17,000 women volunteered to help the children onto trains, provide them with refreshments and ensure they reached their destinations successfully.

Violet knew of the risks involved in moving back to London. It wasn't uncommon for inner-city residents to be completely astonished by how people in the countryside lived their lives. Some found the transition – along with being away from their home comforts – too overwhelming and elected to return to London, well aware of the risks involved. By January 1940 almost half of the evacuees had returned home, mostly because they missed their families too much. The government even produced flyers with Hitler's face on it and emblazoned with the slogan, 'take them back, take them back' across the top. It was meant to serve as a warning to parents who decided to bring their children back to London.

The Kray family's situation was a little different from the average East Ender though; the twins' dad, Charlie, was ordered to report to the Tower Of London for duty, but he didn't want to go to war, so for the years that ensued, he was regularly in hiding or on the run.

In a bid to avoid the police, Charlie lived in Camberwell during this time. He made regular visits back to Vallance Road and on two occasions he was in the house when the police came in to question the family about his whereabouts; he hid in a cupboard and under the table.

This area of Bethnal Green was known as Deserters' Corner during the war, because so many men who were called up to fight didn't go. There are conflicting views on why the men of this area chose not to go to war, but most say it's because they just didn't care for the law.

The air-raid sirens would often sound in this part of London, and the Kray family would hide under railway arches near Vallance Road. Their grandfather, John Lee, was known to put on little variety performances under the arches to keep everybody amused.

The war ended when the twins were 11 and they were finally able to go to Daniel Street School, which is now Green Spring Academy, Shoreditch. They would regularly get into scraps at school and eventually they asked their older brother, Charlie, to teach them some boxing moves.

At this point, Charlie was enlisted in the Navy. Violet allowed the boys to use one of the bedrooms as a sparring room. In a house that was devoid of space, this sort of mentality goes a long way to show that Violet would do anything for her children; including turning one of her bedrooms into a boxing ring. The local children used to flood to the Krays' makeshift gym, some of them – including the Gill Brothers and Charlie Page – would later turn professional.

Without prompting, various interviewees have said to me: 'When you grow up in the East End you either become a boxer or a villain.' Of course, this isn't strictly true, but a number of famous boxers – and famous villains – came out of the East End.

The pair admired villains from the East End's past, which included local gangster Jimmy Spinks. Jimmy Spinks' funeral was such a huge affair, which is said to have only been eclipsed by Ronnie Kray's some forty years later. The pair's biggest idols, though, were Dodger Mullins and Wassle Newman, and the Krays eventually went down a similar path to this Bethnal Green pair.

Just like the Krays, Dodger Mullins and Wassle Newman were known to only fight their own kind – which doesn't include women, children and old people. Contradictory to the Krays' praise for the pair, in John Pearson's book *The Profession Of Violence*, one of his interviewees alleged that, 'Dodger got fed up with one bird he lived with an' threw her out the window.'

While writing this, I've been inundated with stories that start with 'my friend told me…' and as I dig deeper, it's evident that every single gangster of the East End's underworld had groups of people following them that either vilify or verify their stories. The truth is that we'll never truly know whether or not Dodger Mullins threw a woman out of the window, all we can do is speculate into the characters of these villains of East End's past.

Although the childhood of Ronnie and Reggie had spates of fighting, it was generally a common childhood of the time. I mentioned in the introduction how proud everybody was of their houses in the East End and the Krays were no exception. Violet's home was known to be spotless. She kept the house clean, food on the table and always made sure the boys looked presentable; no easy feat for somebody with very little money coming in each month.

But, as the scrappy children turned into teenagers, slowly but surely things started to change. Aged 12, Ron got into trouble for firing a slug gun out the window of a train; but even still, it was hardly a sign of things to come.

Aged 16, the pair were arrested after a fight outside Barry's Dance Hall in Hackney and went up to the Old Bailey on a GBH charge. The case ended up being dismissed as a result of lack of evidence. This was just the start of their long and arduous relationship with the law and Vallance Road quickly became popular with the police – and then the army.

Another run in with the law on Bethnal Green Road came when they were aged 17. A police officer pushed Ron Kray to move him and a group of his friends, including Reggie, on. Ron punched the police officer, and ended up in the back of a police car. To ensure Reggie didn't leave his brother at the police station alone, he also punched the police officer.

Having conducted various interviews and read numerous books, including stories from the pair themselves, Reggie jumping to Ron's defence was quite a regular occurrence. Ron would frequently act without real consideration for his actions, and Reggie would always be there to back him up.

Compulsory military service didn't end until November 1960, so when the Kray twins came of age, they were called up to serve in the Royal Fusiliers. At first, they liked the idea; they'd be physical training instructors and they'd be able to hone their boxing skills. When they arrived at the Tower Of London, though, they quickly realised they wouldn't get a choice in what part they played in the army.

So began two years of dodging the army, spending time in detention centres and getting into trouble with the police. The pair had to spend some time away from Vallance Road during this time – because the police *and* the army were watching it like hawks.

## *178 Vallance Road*

Between 1952 and 1954, the pair spent most of their time on the run or in jail. They were caught and brought back to the barracks – but then escaped – a couple of times. They did a bit of unlicensed boxing during this time, but they were beginning to get a reputation. The boxing world preferred that boxers kept a low profile outside of the ring, but the Kray twins were forever making the headlines of East End newspapers – and not in a positive way.

After they escaped from Canterbury barracks in 1953, the British Army finally kicked the pair out. Ron described this time in his life as a victory; not only had they been able to leave the army, they'd also made friends with criminals during their time at Wormwood Scrubs and Shepton Mallet.

# Chapter 2

# Wood Close School

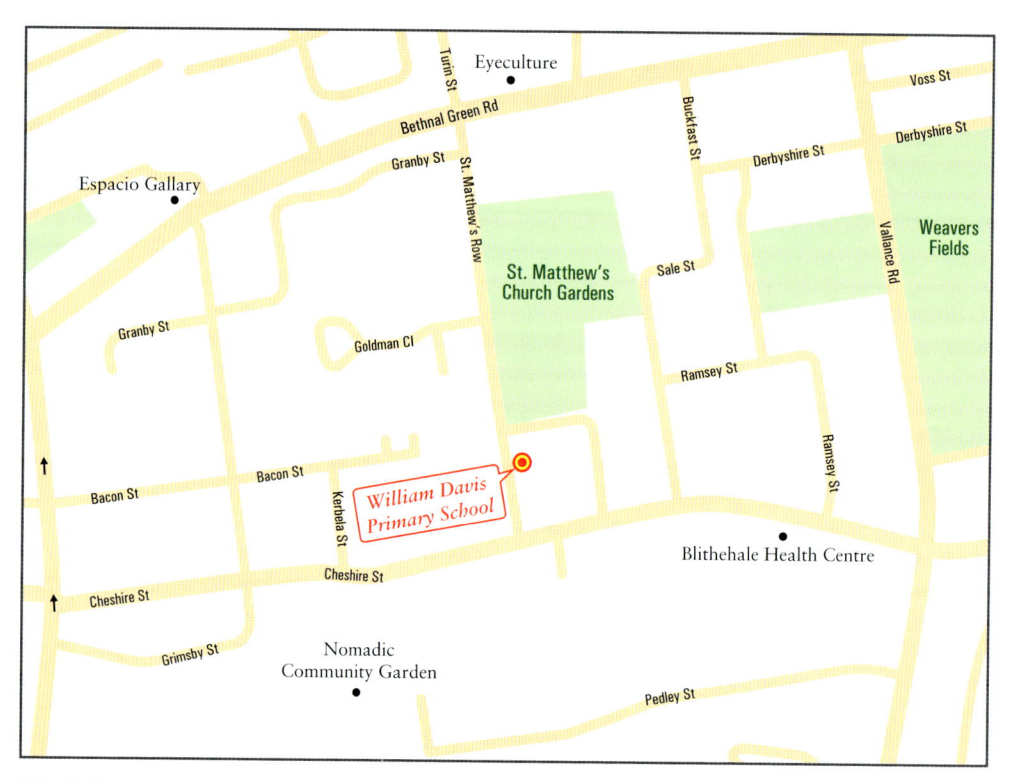

*Wood Close School (now known as William Davis Primary School) where Ronnie and Reggie Kray went to primary school.*

**Where?**
Wood Close School
33 Wood Close
Cheshire Street
Bethnal Green
E2 6DT

**Why?**
This was the first of two schools the Krays went to.

*Wood Close School*

**How to get there:**
The school is within close proximity to Vallance Road. From there, walk back to the crossroads, do a right turning onto Cheshire Street. Wood Close School – which is now known as William Davis Primary School – can be found by taking the third right onto Wood Close. If you are planning on going directly to Wood Close School, Bethnal Green Station is the nearest overground station. From there, walk along the B135 towards Shoreditch. At the crossroads, go straight onto Cheshire Street and take the third right onto Wood Close.

For every child born in the same era as the Krays, school was a very different experience because it was secondary to the war. They only attended the school for one year before the war started and although they still attended while the war was going on, as many pupils during the Second World War would attest, the experience was somewhat different to a normal education. Their start to life was made a little more difficult, too, because they contracted diphtheria aged 3.

Now routinely immunised against, diphtheria was easily spread during the first half of the twentieth century. People were living within close proximity to each other, many of whom were also unable to sanitise themselves properly. There was a large rise in bacterial infections as well as headlice and scabies among young children during this time. Many people – who were young pupils at the time – say it was because their regular school nurse checks had been stopped because nurses were required elsewhere during the war.

Aside from their bout of illness, Ronnie and Reggie were content at Wood Close School. They have spoken very little about their experience, but mentioned that they remember sleeping on camp beds during rest periods.

Other pupils who went to school around Bethnal Green at the same time speak frequently of how their school experience was tainted with the constant threat of war. Children in the East End of London weren't taught traditional subjects; instead, it would be typical to have a day interspersed with air-raid shelter drills. Each time a drill sounded, the pupils would have to make their way to an air-raid shelter and play out the whole dreaded experience time and time again in preparation for the real event.

This time would have been tricky to navigate for Violet. Charlie, the twins' older brother, would have enjoyed his first few years of school with milk tokens and free school dinners, perks that were afforded to the poorest students. However, once the war started, this was taken away along with the school nurse.

Their teachers said they were good and respectable children, and although they got into the occasional scrap, they were no different to any other East End children of the time. It certainly wasn't an indication of things to come at that age. Their teachers, however, were extremely overworked. Male teachers were conscripted into the armed forces and so class sizes quickly grew. The combination of overworked teachers and undernourished children proved difficult for all involved and, unsurprisingly, the level of education decreased.

Reggie had one bad experience in the first years of his life, and until the twins wrote the book *Our Story*, he'd never spoken about it publicly.

It happened on Cheshire Street, a busy road not far from Vallance Road. Reggie, who was 8, and his 9-year-old friend Alf, used to help a local bread van driver by starting up his engine each morning. Reggie would also help loading the bread onto the van and the driver would pay him a few pence a week.

Alf asked Reggie to join him in the van when he was turning on the ignition. For a laugh, Alf turned on the ignition and put the van into gear, not realising that it might move.

It shot backwards and hit an air-raid shelter. There were loud screams, so the pair jumped out to see what was going on. A little boy had been crushed between the van and the air-raid shelter. Reg recalls the accident in his book by saying he 'realised immediately that the boy was dead.'

The van driver asked the pair not to say it was Alf who started the van, or else the driver would lose his job. The pair were called as witnesses at Poplar Town Hall and told the inquest that they'd messed around with the gears but not started the engine. A verdict was recorded as accidental death. Reggie goes on to describe it as his 'saddest memory of all'.

Wood Close School is now called William Davis Primary School and still operates out of the same building as in 1938. This building survived through the Blitz in 1940, which was a remarkable feat given that much of the East End was badly hit. Incendiary devices, which were used en masse on 'Black Saturday' – the worst day of bombings on 7 September 1940 – could cause an irreparable amount of damage, especially to old buildings. A German bomber could hold up to 700 of these devices; they were held in canisters and when dropped, the canisters would open, dropping dozens of them into the sky.

This became a problem for old buildings like those found in the East End, because the small devices would get lodged in roofs, making it hard for firefighters to get to them before they caused damage.

# Chapter 3

# Daniel Street School

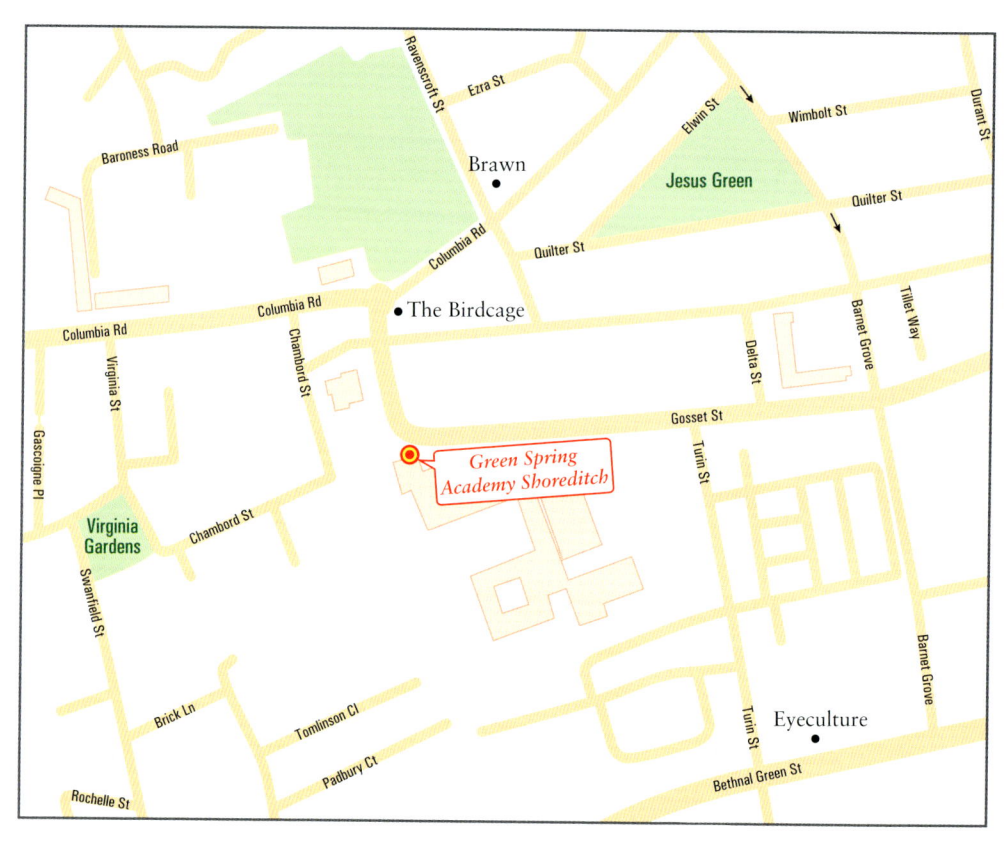

*Daniel Street School (now known as Green Spring Academy) where Ronnie and Reggie went to secondary school.*

**Where?**
Daniel Street School
Gosset Street
Bethnal Green
London
E2 6NW

## Daniel Street School

**Why?**
After Wood Close School, the twins went to secondary school at Daniel Street School.

**How to get there:**
Daniel Street School is now called Green Spring Academy. The easiest way to get there is to get off of the train at Hoxton and make your way towards Hackney Road by making a right as you come out of the station and then a left onto Cremer Street at the end of the road. At the end of Cremer Street, turn right onto Hackney Road and follow it round. Turn left at Colombia Road (if you're visiting on a Sunday, Colombia Road Flower Market is certainly worth a detour). Head straight on Colombia Road until you reach Gosset Street at the roundabout. Turn right and you'll see Green Spring Academy directly in front of you.

Following their time at Wood Close School, they attended Daniel Street School from ages 11-16. It was during these years that their penchant for crime started to take shape. They were regularly involved in playground scraps but most of their fights took place outside of the school gates. At the time, they were also regularly attending Repton Boxing Club and continually improving their game.

One morning, Reggie got in a fight with a boy older – and bigger – than him. He ended up with a black eye, which is one of the reasons Violet let them have a boxing ring inside the house, encouraging them to box properly rather than fight on the streets.

As well as regularly attending school, Ronnie and Reggie joined a youth club nearby to their house on Bethnal Green Road. It was run by a man named Reverend Hetherington. Although they never went to his church, they would often do odd jobs for him. It was Reverend Hetherington who spoke up on behalf of Reggie when he shot slug-gun pellets out of a train window on the way home from Chingford. He also spoke on behalf of both of them when they were arrested for GBH (grievous bodily harm) after they got in a fight outside a nightclub in Hackney.

Many people have fond memories of Daniel Street School; the children were encouraged to box and play football – which suited Ronnie and Reggie particularly well. The team was rather popular in those days and won almost every inter-school trophy and cup.

Teachers who have spoken about them have always said they were fine to deal with as long as you knew how to handle them. Ronnie, particularly, talked in depth about some of the teachers he respected at Daniel Street School and how well they'd handled the twins.

It's clear that Ronnie and Reggie felt more at home here than they ever did during their short spells in Suffolk after the evacuation took place. Although Ronnie went back to Suffolk regularly as he got older, during the war there was a real divide between inner-city and country children. Ronnie and Reggie's experiences of leaving for Suffolk aren't widely documented, and given how quickly they came back after they were evacuated, it's unlikely their experiences shaped their futures in any way.

It is, however, fair to say that the turmoil of the war affected an entire generation of children in one way or another. For many, secondary school defines a teenager – it's a time when many of their beliefs and ideologies become ingrained. For this particular generation though, school was seen as a distraction from the bigger picture; it was continually jolted and lacked any real curriculum and the lack of structure didn't suit the Krays' personalities – hence the ever-increasing penchant for fighting.

Children who were evacuated speak of how they recalled 'punch ups' with locals and that many of the country children believed that those who were evacuated were dirty, lice-ridden and badly behaved. This short stint in the country would've been tough on the twins, as well as Violet. Daniel Street School was perhaps the first chance they had to start to live like normal teenagers.

The school has changed dramatically since Ronnie and Reggie were pupils. There is a large extension to the right of the building, created to accommodate the needs of modern education. The main body of the school, an impressive three-storied, dark-brick building with large white Georgian windows, still looks the same.

The name of the school, however, has changed on numerous occasions. As it stands, the school is called Green Spring Academy. The school recently made the news after four pupils travelled to Syria to join ISIS as Jihadi brides from there. It has continued to make headlines for intimidation and exam-fixing claims.

The Kray twins weren't the only pupils of public interest who went to the school. Comedian Micky Flanagan also went there. He left aged 15 with no qualifications, but later went on to get a degree aged 29.

# Chapter 4

# Repton Boxing Club

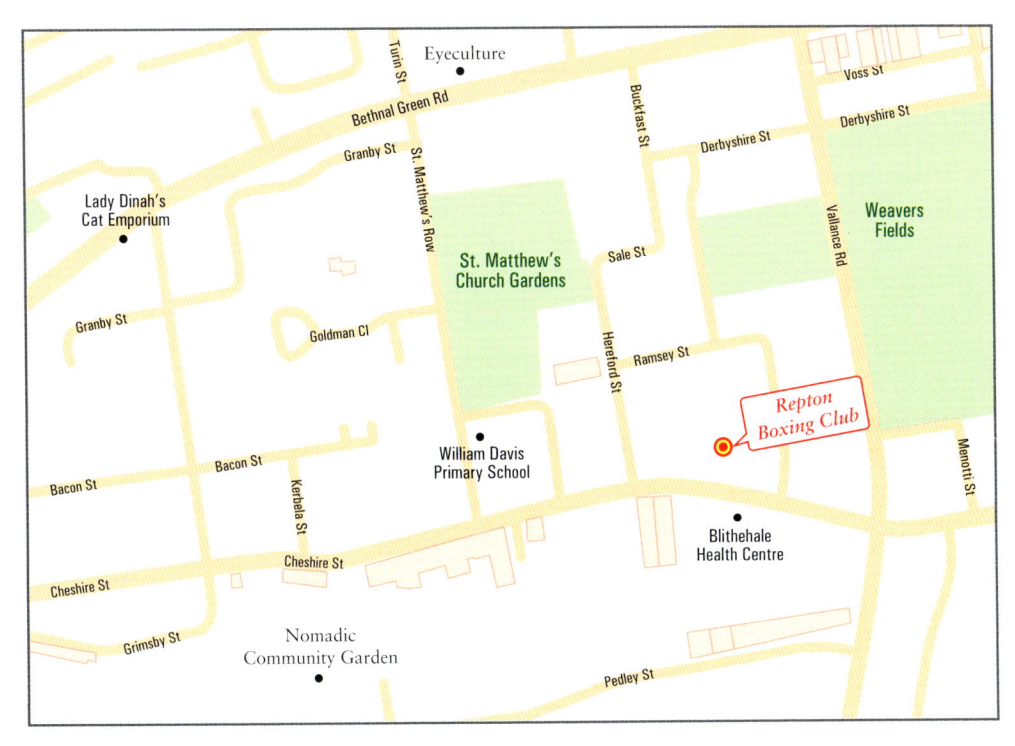

*Repton Boxing Club.*

**Where?**
Repton Boxing Club
The Bath House
116 Cheshire Street
Bethnal Green
London
E2 6EG

**Why?**
This famous boxing gym is where the twins enhanced their amateur boxing careers.

**How to get there:**
Repton Boxing Club is still in the same building as it was when Ronnie and Reggie boxed there. It's a short walk away from many of the Kray twins' most frequented spots. At Bethnal Green Station walk right towards Cheshire Street. At the crossroads continue straight and you will see Repton Boxing Club on your right behind a black gate. The green 'Repton Boxing Club' sign at the front is hard to miss.

London's oldest boxing gym was established in 1884 and is still in operation today. Growing up, the twins spent a lot of time here, as well as in their home boxing ring.

Cheshire Street is a stone's throw away from the now trendy side of Shoreditch. From this location, you could be at the likes of Shoreditch House and Boxpark in minutes. The home of the popular East End Flea Market, Brick Lane, runs south of Cheshire Street and the road that runs alongside it is none other than Vallance Road. You can walk from Brick Lane to Vallance Road in eight minutes.

There has always been something of a spill-over from Brick Lane onto Cheshire Street. The streets were as full in the 1950s and '60s as they are now on a Sunday during the market. It hasn't, though, stopped Repton Boxing Club's impressive growth.

Boxing has always been a popular sport in working-class communities. Some of the residents of the East End at the time say it was because there was no need to buy a kit or any equipment; you could just turn up and box. Others said it was because it was one of the few sports that gave working-class men the chance at fame. Regardless, the working-class preoccupation with boxing in the 1950s is still very much alive today.

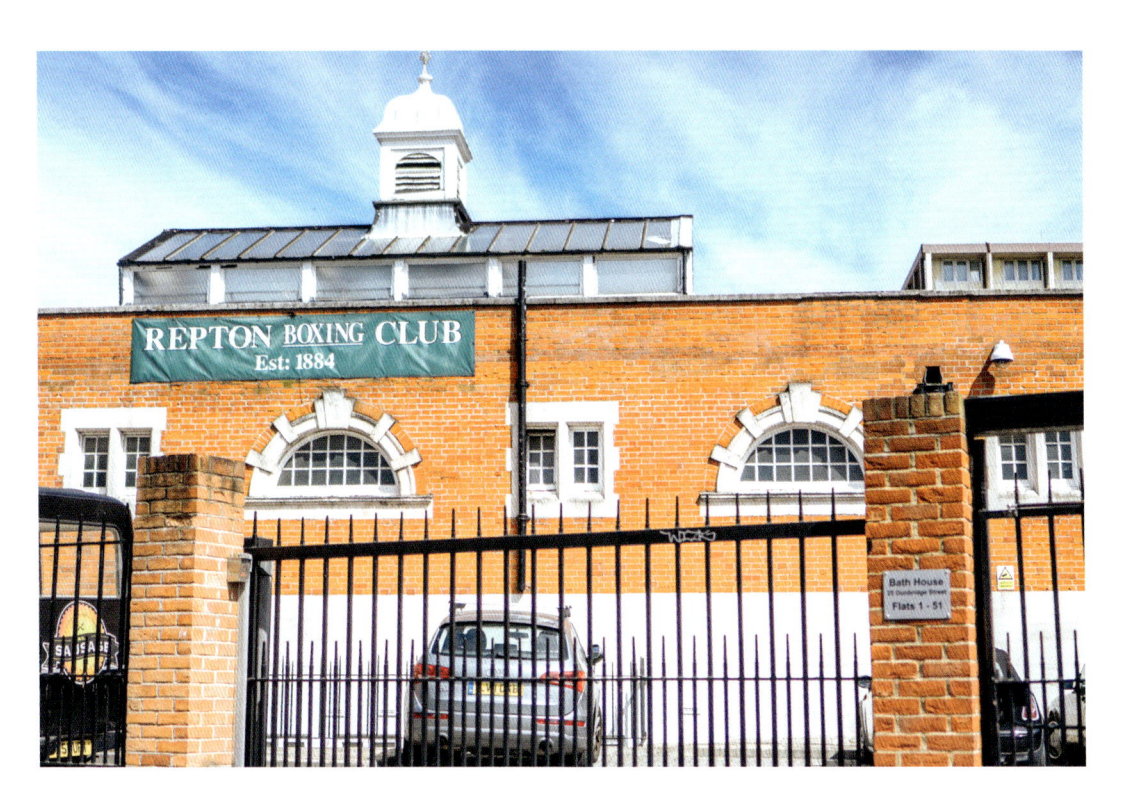

*Repton Boxing Club*

REPTON
BOXING CLUB
ENTRANCE

ENTRANCE
REPTON
BOXING CLUB
WARNING
PRIVATE PROPERTY
UNAUTHORISED
VEHICLES WILL BE
CLAMPED

## Repton Boxing Club

Many people – some of whom still box at Repton Boxing Club and the like, believe that boxing clubs are a refuge for people in poor communities. They're often placed in deprived areas with little or no local amenities. In many cases, and this is still apparent today, boxing clubs are in areas where high-streets and other communal hubs are now mostly shut.

Boxing is also seen as a way to control the violence. Ronnie and Reggie fought in the streets around Vallance Road with bare knuckles; in fact, many European fighters were known to be wary of British boxers because they were unafraid of conflict. In later years, Ronnie and Reggie used to allow boxers to drink in their clubs for free. This attitude goes some way to show just how integral and well-respected the sport was in their lives.

The club is situated within a former Victorian Bath House; the ceiling is high with a glass roof breathing light onto the boxing ring. The high ceiling and windows make the place seem atmospheric whether it's bustling with people or broodingly empty.

The building has a large gated car park at the front of it, which in the crammed streets surrounding Shoreditch makes it feel quite regal. There's something special about this place, and perhaps that's one of the reasons it has stayed open for so many years. It has been home to so many great boxers from Audley Harrison to Maurice Hope and many, many more.

The boxing club was originally established as part of Repton Boys' Club in 1884 by Repton Public School, a co-independent school for boarding and day students based in Repton, Derbyshire. Boarders will currently pay around £35,000 per year to attend this particular establishment. Noteable pupils include Roald Dahl and Jeremy Clarkson, both of whom have openly recalled their time at the school with vehement negativity.

The club was set up and funded in a charitable way to help disadvantaged children and young adults in Bethnal Green. It wasn't out of the ordinary for schools like Repton Public School to fund such endeavours and before long, a number of youth clubs were popping up all across London.

The activities on offer at the club allowed underprivileged youths to experience events and activities that they otherwise wouldn't be able to. Examples of this include, trips outside of London, annual concerts, theatrical performances (often with other local clubs), swimming lessons, cricket and football teams and boxing.

Before long, Oxford House announced its official support for the growing club. Oxford House, which also launched in 1884, was created by Keeble College at the University of Oxford. It was set up so that students and graduates from the university could undertake residential volunteering and learn first-hand about urban poverty. To this day, it's still situated in the heart of Bethnal Green on Derbyshire Street off Bethnal Green Road. The building, which is now Grade II listed, is still the very same one from its years of association with Repton Boys' Club.

The idea behind Oxford House is that it provides practical support to alleviate the impact of poverty in Bethnal Green. It does this by creating youth club projects, offering lawyers to people who can't afford them, offering labour exchanges and providing adult education classes. Repton Boys' Club became part of Oxford House's association after it realised how many working-class youths were being helped by the club. Oxford House advertised the club in its annual report, which only boosted its popularity.

Above and below: *Oxford House is still in operation to this day.*

From the offset, Repton Boys' Club was very sports-focused, and by the twentieth century, it had gained quite the reputation around the East End. Ronnie and Reggie were lucky to have this institution on their doorstep and the pair took full advantage.

It was at this point that Repton Boys' Club began focusing on boxing more exclusively; it had a reputation as a great place to train, even at this point in its history. There was a thin line between boxing and fighting though, and the club started to pick up headlines for the wrong reasons. As a result, Repton Public School announced its withdrawal of support in 1971. At the time, Oxford House was temporarily closed and so wasn't involved in the decision.

It didn't matter at this point, though. The club had gained such a following that it simply changed its name to Repton Boxing Club and continued to operate as a boxing gym. It is considered to be the oldest boxing club in the United Kingdom and has produced over 500 champions in both amateur and professional boxing. Some famous members, according to Oxford House, include John H. Stracey and Maurice Hope, as well as Olympians Sylvester Mittee, Audley Harrison and Tony Cesay.

The Kray twins' route into boxing is easy to map. They came from a family of fighters. John Lee, their grandad who used to entertain them under the railway arches during the war, was known as the Southpaw Cannonball. He got this name because he could hit so hard with his left hand. They grew up with stories of East End fighting ingrained into them.

In 1948, aged 15 and after a number of qualification fights, Reggie won the London Schoolboys' Boxing Championship. He was almost unbeaten as an amateur and won seven out of seven fights as a lightweight.

He quit after his seventh fight, largely due to the bad press the pair had started to generate. As boxing is a violent sport, managers and promoters preferred boxers to have an outstanding record outside of the boxing ring. The Kray twins were making headlines for the wrong reasons and this put the world of boxing off them.

Reggie was widely known as the better boxer of the two, but Ron boxed as well. As a professional, Ron won four out of six fights as a welterweight. Ron regularly said that he thought Reggie could have gone all the way and that he held him back in scraps outside the boxing ring.

That marked the beginning and end of Ronnie and Reggie's boxing careers, although they continued to be keen fighters outside the boxing ring.

Repton Boxing Club is world-renowned and a name within its own right. Many similar boxing rings have since opened their doors to box-fit classes and beginner lessons to get in some extra money, but not Repton Boxing Club. The club is for high-level, competitive boxers and makes extra money from its use as a location for films, such as *Lock, Stock and Two Smoking Barrels*, and from music videos for the likes of Plan B and Take That. The retro look and feel of the place lends itself well for filming of this kind.

The club relies on charitable donations to keep running and receives no funding from the government or local authorities.

# Chapter 5

# G. Kelly Pie & Mash

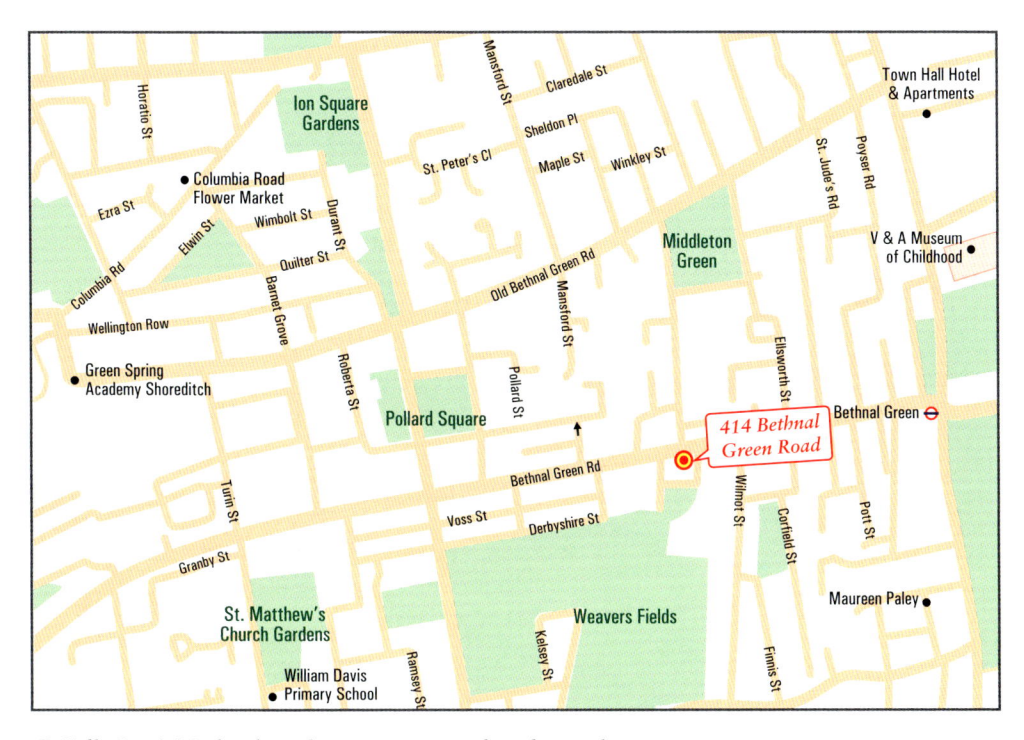

*G. Kelly Pie & Mash, where the twins were regulars during their younger years.*

**Where?**
414 Bethnal Green Road
London
E2 0DJ

and,

526 Roman Road
Bow
London
E3 5ES

**Why?**
No tour of the East End of London is complete without a stop at a Pie & Mash shop. This one was regularly frequented by the Kray twins.

**How to get there:**
The shop on Bethnal Green Road is a short walk from Bethnal Green Underground station. When coming out of the station, simply head along Bethnal Green Road to number 414. If you'd prefer to walk along Mile End Road to the second of the G. Kelly Pie & Mash shops, it's in the opposite direction. Walk straight along Mile End Road until you reach 526. The walk is about 1.1 miles. The Pie & Mash shop on Bethnal Green Road is nearer to other key Kray twins locations.

The shops have a rich history. On their website it reads:

> In 1915, Samuel Robert Kelly opened a shop in Bethnal Green. He had been working as a tram driver but an injury forced him to give up this work. He decided to invest some compensation money he had received into a business and opened his first Eel and Pie shop in Bethnal Green Road. He and his wife Matilda had four children Samuel, George, Matilda and Joe, who all went on to open eel and pie shops.

Pie and mash is an institution in the East End of London and as most East Londoners would attest, G. Kelly Pie & Mash is the pinnacle. The famous shop has two outlets, one in Bethnal Green Road and one in Roman Road; both of which were regularly visited by the Krays and members of The Firm.

Pie and mash shops are still popular in London, Kent and Essex nowadays, although not quite on the scale they once were. It would be typical for East Enders to regularly visit the pie and mash shop for their dinner, perhaps once a week – perhaps even more often. We've established by now that Ronnie and Reggie were very much part of the working-class community of London. This community favoured cheap and easy meals that were plentiful. Many of the residents of Bethnal Green would have had labour-intensive jobs and would certainly have worked up an appetite; pie and mash ticked all of the boxes.

The pie was a favourite among the working classes long before Ronnie and Reggie were born. The thick crust lining the pie would be handled by workers who had dirty hands. Nowadays we eat the thick crust lining the outsides, but in the past, that was used to protect the filled pie from dirt and grime.

This, alongside jellied eels, was known as workers' food. Eels were one of the few fish that could survive in the heavily polluted River Thames, so they too became a popular staple in pie and mash shops across the East End.

When Ronnie and Reggie were young, they were regularly sent to the shop on Bethnal Green Road by Violet to pick up pie and mash for the family. On G. Kelly's 100 year anniversary, the owner recalled the twins used to unscrew the vinegar lids so that the customers would unwittingly pour it all over their dinner. His dad used to send them home regularly without dinner.

When Ronnie and Reggie died many years later, G. Kelly's were asked if they minded the funeral procession pausing outside the shop, and they happily obliged. The procession did this to a few choice places around the East End as a mark of respect to the places Ronnie and Reggie used to love.

The shops which are still in operation today originally belonged to George Kelly. G. Kelly on Roman Road opened in 1939 and was bought by his brother-in-law Bill Kingdon in the mid-1950s. Bill's daughter, Sue, and her family now run the shops. Like G. Kelly's, most of the pie and mash shops in London were family-run and as such, were passed down the family for generations.

Before pie and mash shops started popping up across East London, East Enders were able to get their fix from the local pie and eel man. These street sellers would sell pea soup and hot eels.

Dating back to 1871, Henry Mayhew, a social historian, wrote about his experiences of the occupations of the poor. He documented the state of working people in London for a series of articles for the newspaper *The Morning Chronicle*. Later, though, the articles were compiled into a book called *London Labour And The London Poor*, in which Mayhew speaks in detail about the 'London pie men' and how they would roam the streets, visiting taverns and fairs. An interesting tradition was born whereby a coin would be tossed for a pie. If the pie man won, he'd keep the penny and the pie, if the member of the public won, they would take the pie and the penny. Henry Mayhew was absolutely fascinated with this revelation and spoke about it in detail in his articles.

Even then, eels were purchased from Billingsgate Market. This is still a very popular tradition among stall holders and restauranteurs alike. Mayhew believed there could be up to 500 sellers of eels on the streets of London on any given Saturday.

As Mayhew was writing, he had already noticed the rise in pie and mash shops. The pie man trade had been extremely profitable, but when the shops started appearing, this trade died out. The rise in the shops, over what was then the 'traditional pie man' was a welcome change to the locals. Although the pie and eel men said the rise in the shops had an irreparable impact on their business, the locals liked having a shop nearby. At the time, there was a huge rise in population; from Irish immigrants fleeing the famine to refugees fleeing political persecution in Europe. These families, who were living in unimaginable conditions – and without access to cooking facilities – were now able to get warm food cheaply. This had a positive impact on the local community and thus, the pie and mash business flourished.

The shop on Bethnal Green Road was particularly popular with the Krays – and many other East Enders, during the war. It was one of the few shops that managed to stay open. The owners persuaded the Ministry of Food to allow a special quota of food in order to offer home cooked, warm meals to the people of Bethnal Green and the surrounding areas. Many of the people interviewed said this was a real treat and something they remembered fondly.

George Kelly had an entrepreneurial mindset, he continued to grow his business by opening more pie shops in the local area. He also, however, ran a successful eel-supply business. This multi-faceted approach to the business would have certainly played a large part in his success. This entrepreneurial spirit, teamed with the high levels of quality and cleanliness always shown throughout his shops, is probably the reason G. Kelly Pie & Mash has eclipsed much of its competition throughout the years.

To this day pie and mash remains an important part of East End lifestyle. When asked what many Londoners associate with cockneys, the vast majority of them say pie and mash. For a true to life East End experience, these pie and mash shops are not to be missed.

# Chapter 6

# The Regal

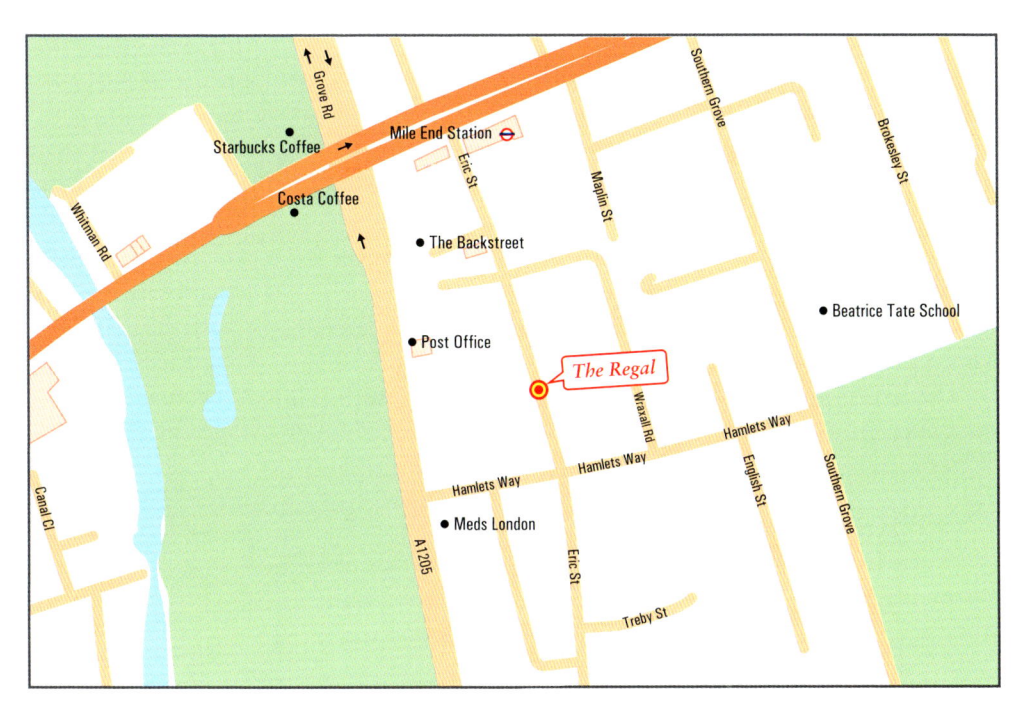

*The Regal, Ronnie and Reggie's first business.*

**Where?**
124 Eric Street
Mile End
London
E3 4SR

**Why?**
This was Ronnie and Reggie's first business, aged just 20 years old.

**How to get there:**
It's easy to get to Eric Street from Mile End Underground station; the supported living facility – which now sits in place of The Regal, is directly behind Mile End

Underground station. Simply leave the station, do a left and then take the first left onto Eric Street. Coopers Court – the supported living facility – is less than a quarter of the way down Eric Street. Although the original building is no longer there, the road and surrounding areas are perfectly intact.

The twins were just 20 years old when they acquired their first business venture: The Regal. The building was run-down and in a particularly undesirable part of London at the time, making the acquisition an inexpensive financial move for them.

Between 1910 and 1940 The Regal had been a 702-seater cinema called Forrest's Electrodrome. Although it changed hands twice in thirty years, it was largely popular with the residents of the East End. By 1940 though it had become dilapidated and was sold to be a working factory and warehouse to serve the war; after that, it became a billiard hall. Ronnie and Reggie came to learn about the unkept hall through word-of-mouth. It was rumoured that small-time gangs were meeting up to discuss their dealings. Having already forayed into the criminal world, the twins were intrigued and decided to visit.

On arrival, it was clear the hall needed work. It was a large, white building with prison-like windows placed sporadically around the one small entrance door. Like many snooker halls still in operation today, the place operated on a no-frills approach. This, in turn, attracted all sorts of unsavoury characters.

The twins' initial plan for the billiard hall was to turn it into a meeting place for their ever-growing gang, The Firm, which was in the beginning stages of formation;

*The Regal*

they were more of a group of friends at the time. At 20, the twins were only dabbling in petty crime, and the extended group were also involved in minor criminal activities.

In the early days, aside from Ronnie, Reggie and their brother, Charlie, The Firm consisted of Tommy Brown, also more commonly known as 'the bear' due to his powerful shoulders and fighting prowess. He was a family friend of the Krays and spent time with Ronnie and Reggie growing up. Over the years, Tommy spent a number of days – with Reggie in particular – sparring in the back garden of 178 Vallance Road and improving Reggie's technique. Tommy assisted the twins by working as a doorman on many of their clubs. When the twins acquired The Regal, though, Tommy was nothing more than a friend and fellow boxer to them. His involvement in The Firm came shortly after their acquisition.

Dickie Morgan was also a key figure in The Firm when it was in its infancy. He was a founding member and lifelong friend of the twins. The three first met while on the run from the army and it was during this time they began their criminal endeavours together. At the time, he was living with his mother just a short walk away from the billiard hall that was to become The Regal. During their run from the army, the twins would often stay at 32 Clinton Road – Dickie's mother's house – and this is how they began frequenting the billiards hall. Opening The Regal was very much a joint venture between the trio.

In the few pictures of Ronnie and Reggie at The Regal which were released to the public, Billy Donovan and Pat Connolly are also featured. Billy Donovan, who played a key role in The Firm in later years, didn't always have a good relationship with the Krays. It's alleged he nearly lost an eye after a fight with Ronnie. It was his silence during the ensuing police involvement that earned him his place in their inner circle. Like Dickie Morgan, Billy Donovan also ended up working on the door of a number of the Krays' clubs.

The final face in the released images is that of Pat Connolly, another founding member of The Firm who played an integral role right until the end of the Krays' reign over the streets of East London. He went on to act as Club Secretary at The Double R Club, but when The Regal was opened, he was just a friend of the twins who shared their mutual love for boxing – and fighting.

There was trouble at The Regal before the Krays took over; local gangs were going in and ripping tables apart, smashing glasses and fighting between themselves. It meant that residents from the local area were terrified to set foot in there, which impacted on the takings. The owner bought a large Alsatian dog to deter the gangs, but it didn't keep them away. The perpetrators would throw fireworks over the counter, which eventually drove the dog to insanity.

A number of people claimed that the Krays ordered the local tearaways to cause havoc at The Regal so they could go in and take it over. They regularly denied this rumour, claiming that they didn't have enough clout at the time and that the problems at The Regal started way before the pair had come of age.

It wasn't long before the manager started paying Ronnie and Reggie £5 per week to oversee the day-to-day running of the place. They were on a one-month probation, which was quickly extended. The role they played included warding off more established gangs who were already operating a protection racket in the area. At this point, the pair had only dabbled in protection money so this was no doubt an eye-opening experience for them and perhaps a lesson in how to go about demanding this money for their future ventures.

The gang in question was a Maltese group who were demanding protection money, so the Krays went straight for them with knives. According to Reggie, they never saw the gang again.

The violence attracted by the billiard hall slowly stopped after the twins were made the legal tenants of the property in 1954. In fact, they'd become something of a feature of the place. Reggie – who had a keen eye for interiors and would go on to design all of their ventures – redecorated the place and local criminals began to flock to it for no other reason than to visit Ronnie and Reggie.

They had a three-year lease and borrowed some money which bought fourteen second-hand tables and paid for Reggie's redecoration. They were paying £5 a month in rent, so as soon as the place became busy again, they weren't short of profits.

Ronnie and Reggie credit The Regal as the place that started The Firm. At that age, they liked a drink, they liked to go out, and they had more money than most of their associates of the same age. This afforded them a large crowd of eager followers. Some of them were petty thieves, others were more high-profile.

Given the size of The Regal, it wasn't long before thieves and other criminals were asking the Krays to hide their loot in exchange for a percentage in whatever they

*The Regal*

were hiding. They revelled in this; Reggie believed the hiding of stolen goods is what started Ronnie's obsession with guns.

The protection racket hadn't quite disappeared, though. Another gang from Poplar arrived demanding money and the Krays beat them up quite badly. It was in this exchange that Ronnie and Reggie realised the potential a successful protection racket could have.

The Regal has been completely demolished since then to make way for a care home called Cooper's Court. It can be found opposite The Wentworth Arms at the end of Eric Street.

# Chapter 7

# Chris' Hairdressers

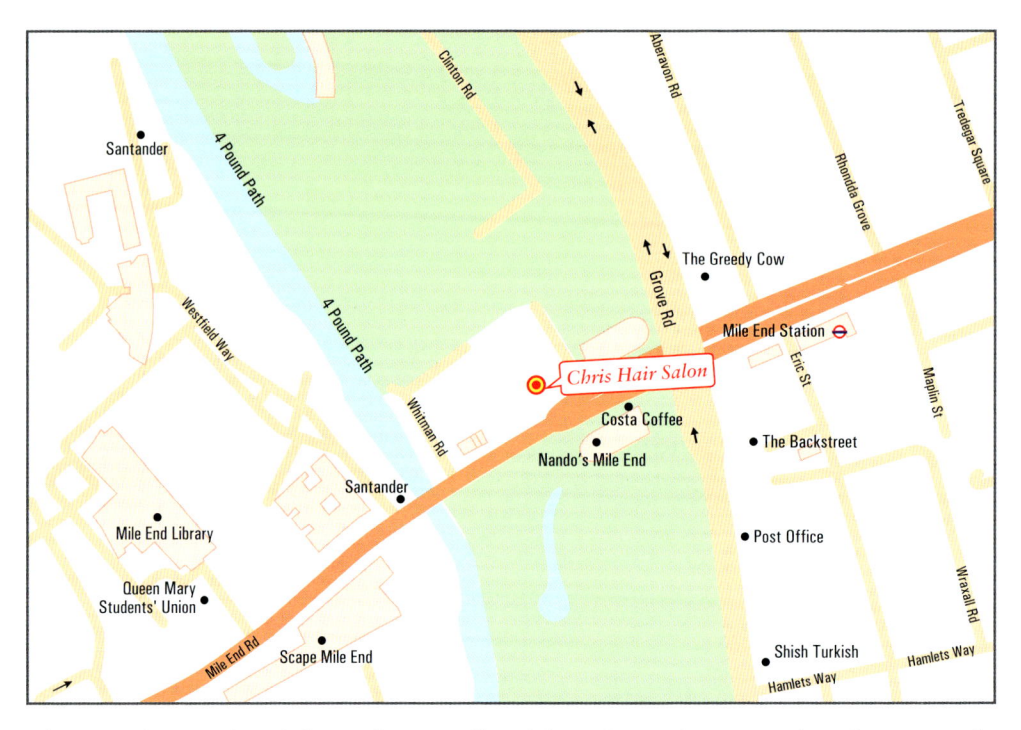

*Chris' Hairdressers; the only luxury the twins allowed themselves as they were making their way up the ladder in the criminal underworld.*

**Where:**
371 Mile End Road
Stepney
London
E1 4NT

**Why:**
The Kray twins' slick look became iconic over the years. Chris' Hairdressers was one of their best kept secrets.

*Chris' Hairdressers*

**How to get there:**
This shop is another stop on Mile End Road and is situated nearby the site where The Regal used to stand. Chris' Hairdressers is a short walk from Mile End Underground station. Take a left on Mile End Road as you leave the station and walk for approximately three minutes (0.1 miles). The shop is across the road from Mile End Underground station, but you may find you get a better vantage point for photographs on the other side of the road.

In The Krays' book *Our Story*, Reggie mentions that the only real luxury the pair had – when they started to make money aged around 21 – was a hairdresser, my great-grandad Chris, who would regularly cut the pair's hair. Reggie said he got this idea from an American gangster film.

Throughout their lives, they were known for their dark, slicked back hair. This was very much the style of the generation. In the UK in the '50s and '60s, men almost exclusively wore suits. Some fashion blogs have tied the Krays' style to that of Italian gangsters of the time. Either way, the pair's style was always impeccable.

The attire of the 1950s had an air of sophistication about it. Men didn't keep suits for special occasions; instead, on an average night out, men would be dressed in suits, formal shoes, ties, tie clips and pocket squares. Icons of the time ranged from the ever-suave Frank Sinatra to teddy boys. Colours were kept quite traditional and suits were typically worn in three colours: blue, grey and brown.

During a more casual day, men would wear a 'sports coat' and slacks. Nowadays, this outfit looks very much like a suit, but in the 1950s there was a clear distinction. A sports coat was a jacket that differed in colour to the trousers. Invariably, a sports jacket would feature some sort of plaid pattern. A hat was also a popular option, particularly in the summer. In the summer, men would also opt for lighter fabric, in both weight and colour. Many men of the 1950s would select a light-brown or dark-beige suit for the summer months.

The '50s-look of suits and cocktail dresses went down in history as being the golden age of fashion for many, with this sleek look resurfacing many times over the years. At this point in time women were mostly homemakers, but in 1947 Christian Dior's bold new collection was the beginning of the trend of women shopping. A full skirt and padded bust was meant to accentuate a woman's tiny waist. A popular item of clothing among women was a full-skirted swing dress in simple cottons and small prints or plaid. It had large pockets and three-quarter-length sleeves with a matching fabric belt. A light petticoat would be worn underneath, and an apron over the top to keep it clean. The twins' mother, Violet, didn't subscribe to this trend; in the '50s and '60s she was seen wearing semi-fitted midi-length skirts and light, loose-fitting jumpers quite regularly. The colour palette and patterns on her clothing, though, were very in-keeping with the era.

Although the twins' hair has been documented widely on fashion blogs and in 60s-based 'get the look' articles, the hairdresser behind this famous style was scarcely mentioned. The reason behind this is because he wasn't part of the gangster underworld. Although, arguably he 'knew too much' at times, he didn't get involved in The Firm and instead kept a modest, but rather busy, shop.

The shop's original home was on Burdett Road; a busy 'A' road linking Mile End Road to East India Dock Road. This is where the Kray twins went, before Cypriot-born Chris Kyriacou was asked to meet them at various locations while they were on the run.

His stepdaughter, Pat King, recalls 'My Mum would regularly moan about their set-up. She never had a problem with them but we all knew they were gangsters. She'd say to Chris "I hope you're not paying them any protection money."'

Chris never paid the pair protection money, like many of the other local businesses on Burdett Road. They struck up something of a friendship over the years and the twins' offered Chris protection for free. Chris – who we affectionately called Fafa from a young age – passed away a few years back, but not before he shared many, many stories of his experiences with the Kray twins.

Like many of the people I interviewed, Chris had nothing negative to say about the Krays. He, like the other interviewees, was perhaps one stage removed from the more violent side of The Firm.

He remembers a time when he had them in the shop on Burdett Road:

> I was just finishing up somebody's hair and I had Ronnie and Reggie in the waiting room. My stepdaughter ran in with a cut thumb, it was pouring with blood. They were straight to her and told me I should go to the hospital right away to get it sorted. I shut the shop and they didn't get their hair cut that day.

This is ultimately the response that anybody with a conscience would have. But, many books written about the Kray twins would argue that the pair didn't have a conscience, full-stop.

Chris' Hairdressers can now be found on Mile End Road, with the original fronting that it had when it was frequented by Ronnie and Reggie Kray. Chris moved the hairdressers because that area of Burdett Road was being knocked down and rebuilt. But when that was occurring, the Kray twins were on the run.

Unlike their teenage years of running from the army, this time, they were on the run from the police. Throughout their lives, Ronnie and Reggie were frequently on the run from, or avoiding, the police but one of the first times it got a bit more serious was in 1955.

At this point, Ron was around two years into a battle with mental health; a battle that would last a lifetime. It was in Canterbury Barracks two years previous to this that people started to notice his mental health declining. He wouldn't wash, he would only shave half of his face and, in his words, he would 'play the fool'. He was certified insane in 1956 – but a little more on that later.

## Chris' Hairdressers

In 1955, Ron shot his first man with a Luger pistol. The man had been threatening a garage owner who paid the Kray twins for protection. The conversation got heated and so Ron shot him in the leg. He managed to get away with it on this occasion by threatening the man he'd shot and giving his wife money to be quiet.

That time, it worked. But a year later when they had a battle with a group of Irish dockers called the Watney Streeters, Ron didn't get so lucky. One of the Watney Streeters, Jackie Martin, was very badly hurt and was happy to name Ron Kray as one of the men who attacked him. By November 1956, aged 23, Ron was in Wandsworth prison for a three-year stint.

Chris found Ron easy to get along with, but he said there was a definite edge to him, that Reggie didn't have: 'He was a bit more unpredictable. When he was in a bad mood, he was quiet and you didn't know how to act. Reggie was more level headed. Ron's moods were very up and down.'

In 1958, shortly after Ron had found out that their beloved Auntie Rose had died of leukaemia, Ron was sent to Long Grove mental hospital near Epsom. He recounts his experience: 'I was in an awful state, thought the bloke in the opposite bed was a dog. I couldn't recognise anyone.'

Reggie had concerns that his brother's mental state would mean he'd be destined to a life in and out of mental hospitals. So, the pair swapped places. Ronnie left the hospital, after swapping his clothes with Reggie. When the doctors returned to his bed, Reggie asked to leave; they couldn't keep him there because they knew immediately he was Reggie Kray and Ron must've already left. This wasn't the first – nor the last – mind trick that they'd play on the authorities.

Ron spent the months that ensued living in a caravan on a farm in Suffolk. This was the first time Chris was driven to visit Ron, so he could have his haircut.

His daughter, Pat King, recalls: 'Every so often a very handsome man, who was later announced as Ron's boyfriend, would come to the door for Chris. Chris would get into the back of his car and return hours later having cut Ron's hair.'

Both Ronnie and Reggie were on the run at numerous times in their lives, but Chris said he would 'most regularly go to Suffolk' for his hairdressing appointments.

# Chapter 8

# The Double R Club

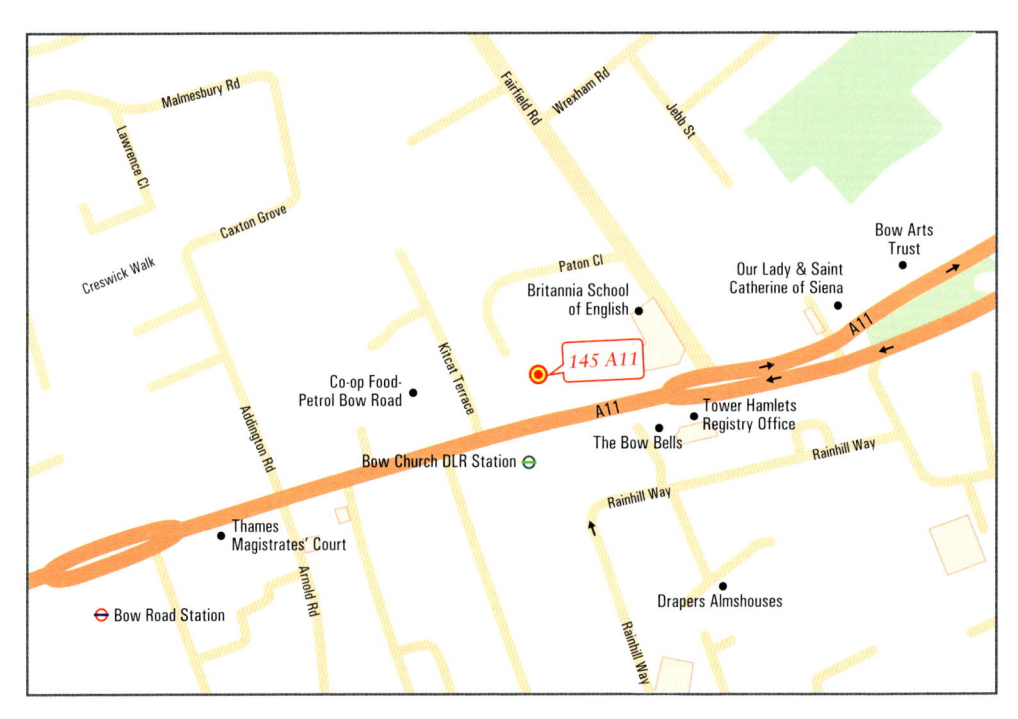

*The Double R Club; one of the most famous clubs the Krays owned.*

**Where?**
145 Bow Road
Bow
London
E3 3AH

**Why?**
The Double R was Ronnie and Reggie's very first nightclub.

**How to get there:**
An Enterprise garage stands in place of The Double R Club now. There are still plenty of reasons to visit this area, though, particularly the grand neo-baroque style building

that used to house Bow Police Station. 145 Bow Road is a very short walk from Bow Road station and an even shorter walk from Bow Church DLR station. From Bow Road station, simply leave the station and head right on Bow Road until you reach the Enterprise Garage. If you're coming out of Bow Church DLR station, the garage is situated almost straight in front of you as you leave the station. Remember to stop for a look at Bow Police Station on the corner of Bow Road and Addington Road.

Ron's time on the run came to an end and eventually he went back to Long Grove voluntarily. In his absence, Reg and his brother Charlie, began to build numerous business ventures. One of the first was a nightclub in Bow called the Double R. Although most of Reggie's business ventures were undertaken alongside his brother Ron, it was well documented that Reggie and Charlie worked well in a partnership.

Reggie missed Ronnie while he was at Long Grove – it was the first time in their lives so far that the pair had been apart for any length of time. In homage to his brother, Double R – a way to build both of their names into the venture – was born.

The Double R needed a lot of work, in its original form it was an empty shop. As well as gathering all of the necessary legal paperwork and licenses, it needed completely redecorating. Charlie and Reggie worked hard together, forming quite the formidable partnership, and officially opened the club on 6 May 1957. As well as the club itself, Reggie and Charlie turned the upstairs into a gym and had the boxer Henry Cooper officially open it.

News of The Double R spread; in many ways, it put Ronnie and Reggie on the wider map. Not only were they making a name for themselves within the Bethnal Green community, but people further afield were beginning to recognise the name Kray. It was during this time that The Firm really developed itself. Tommy Brown, Dickie Morgan, Billy Donovan and Pat Connolly were still part of the group – which grew in numbers after various meetings at The Regal – but it was now more than just a group of friends, it was a gang.

With Ronnie and Reggie's protection business growing rapidly, The Firm's primary crime was extorting money from various local businesses. Aside from that, the gang was also heavily involved in fraud and organised crime. The key areas of operation were Bethnal Green, Mile End, Whitechapel, Bow and Hackney. There were a huge number of local businesses operating out of these areas, and given their close proximity to the more undesirable areas of London, the business owners felt they needed protection. The Firm ensured the businesses were granted protection, but they were also there to collect the money at the end of each week.

During the days of The Double R, The Firm picked up a number of other key members. Albert Donoghue was the first, he went on to play an integral role in the gang until the very end. Albert knew of The Firm through Billy Donovan, who was already very much involved with the day-to-day operations. Billy knew Albert because they were both dating – and ended up married to – sisters. He met the twins a number of times at The Double R because of his close association with Billy, who worked on the door. It wasn't until a little later in the Kray twins' journey, though, that Albert became a fundamental component of The Firm.

*The Krays' London*

While Albert was getting to know the rising stars of the East End, Tommy Brown was making a name for himself as the strong man of The Double R. It's alleged that one night in The Double R, Tommy Brown lifted one disruptive customer by his tie and swung him around the club.

It was also at this point that Leslie Payne started to become a prominent figure among the ever-growing gang. Leslie Payne was on the con-man circuit long before he came across Ronnie and Reggie; he ended up pitching his skills to them in order to get a coveted place in their inner circle. Ronnie was always sceptical of Leslie's involvement within The Firm, but Reggie found his background in the criminal underworld to be quite helpful to their growing organisation. Leslie Payne's experience made him the 'brains' behind the operation. The Firm flourished under his leadership and before long he was seen as Reggie's right-hand man.

The building is no longer standing, instead, there's now an Enterprise car-rental garage in its place. Nowadays, it sits directly opposite to Bow Church DLR station; quite a different scene to that of 1958.

There are still a couple of points of interest on this road, though. The grand neo-baroque style building on the corner of Bow Road and Addington Road which used to be Bow Road Police Station for one. It closed down in recent years as part of the Met Police budget cut, so is no longer operational. When Ronnie was on the run from the police, it was been reported on numerous occasions that he used to walk back and forth outside this police station just to taunt them.

Aside from the police station, there used to be a pub called The Black Swan that sat directly opposite The Double R Club. Albert Donoghue pretended to the police that he was drinking in this pub when in fact he was being shot by Reggie; more detail on that a little later on. This plot of land is also fascinating because of its link to the Zeppelin raid in the First World War. The pub that stood there originally was bombed, causing the deaths of two young girls. There's a popular wartime tale about how the two girls came back as ghosts.

When being interviewed, people from the East End remember the Double R as the main establishment owned by the Kray twins. It marketed itself as a little piece of the West End lifestyle in the East End. Everybody remembered going there; men would wear tailored suits, women would wear cocktail dresses and the music and dancing would last until the early hours. Considering this particular club was only open for three years, that's quite a testament.

It wasn't long until the club started attracting famous faces: Queenie Watts, Barbara Windsor, Jackie Collins and Sybil Burton were regular patrons – to name a few.

At the time, the police were turning a blind eye to Reggie's dealings; the clubs were well run and because the Krays owned it, it didn't attract much trouble. It suited the police not to look into the inner workings of the Double R.

That was, of course, until the introduction of Ronnie Marwood. On 14 December 1958, Ronnie Marwood, a 25-year-old scaffolder, stabbed a police officer outside Grays Dance Hall in Holloway. Marwood said he never intended to use his weapon when the fight broke out, but his actions led to the death of 23-year-old policeman Raymond Henry Summers.

## The Double R Club

Marwood went to Reggie and asked him to hide him from the police. Reggie, not being able to say no to a fellow criminal, decided to help him out. Reggie later said he didn't owe Ronnie Marwood anything, in fact, he barely knew him.

This pattern of behaviour plagued Reggie Kray for his entire life. Interviewees often commented that he was the 'nicer' of the two twins, but that he had an innate need to get involved in other people's criminal activity; and in most cases, that activity involved his brother, Ron.

It was this decision that cost Reggie the Double R. The police offered him a deal: if he told them where Ronnie Marwood was hiding, they'd let him run his clubs without any trouble. When he refused, it wasn't long until the police started digging into the activities of the club. It was shut down shortly afterwards.

Ronnie Marwood ended up turning himself in a month later and was hanged for his crime on 8 May 1959.

There are many rumours surrounding the demise of the Double R Club. While Ronnie and Reggie Kray say it was because of Ronnie Marwood and the intervention by the police, locals at the time said it was because of Ronnie's increasingly unusual behaviour. Ronnie would often bring in Tex The Dwarf, a midget who wore a Texan hat and would ride in on a donkey. Some people loved this act, others felt it was odd.

Either way, the Double R was shut.

# Chapter 9

# E. Pellicci's Cafe

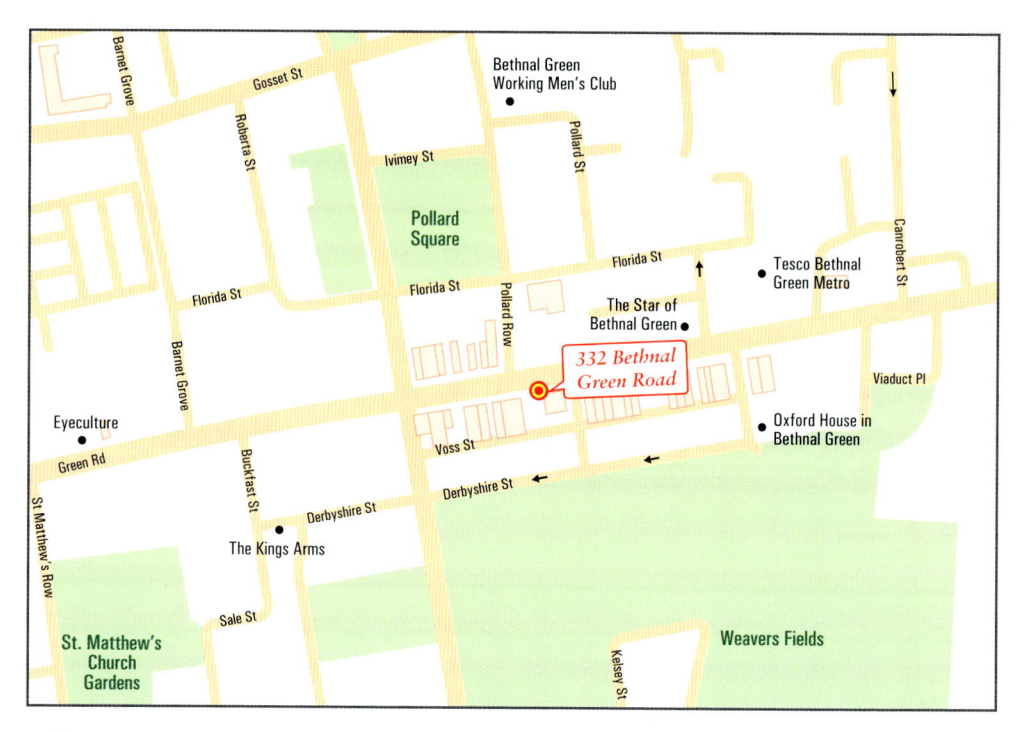

*Pellicci's Cafe; a regular haunt of The Firm.*

**Where?**
332 Bethnal Green Road
London
E2 0AG

**Why?**
Ronnie, Reggie and The Firm would eat breakfast here every morning. Both twins regularly said how much they would love to have one last meal at E. Pellicci's Cafe when they were in prison.

## E. Pellicci's Cafe

**How to get there:**
E. Pellicci's Cafe is another stop along Bethnal Green Road and very close to G. Kelly Pie & Mash. The nearest underground station is Bethnal Green. When getting off at Bethnal Green Underground station you can walk straight down Bethnal Green Road towards Shoreditch. E. Pellicci's Cafe is on your right. It's 0.3 miles along that road and should take around five to seven minutes to walk. Another interesting stop along that route is Oxford House, which funded Repton Boys' Boxing Club for some time. You can find that off Derbyshire Street on the left about ¾ of the way between Bethnal Green Underground station and E. Pellicci's Cafe. It's certainly worth a look because it's a rather impressive building.

This cafe on Bethnal Green Road was opened in 1900 and is still managed by the same family. It's more than a greasy spoon; it has an art-deco feel about it, making it an interesting visit whether you're intrigued by the Kray twins or not.

As well as being a regular spot with the Krays, Pellicci's Cafe was also featured in the most recent film about the duo – *Legend*. The staff are more than happy to tell customers about the shoot and the food is far superior to many other London cafes; the plethora of celebrity guests, from David Schwimmer to Frank Lampard, certainly validates the quality of Pellicci's.

A lot of the Krays' lives seem to centre around a three-mile radius of Vallance Road. This wasn't unique to the Kray family; almost all people from the East End lived, worked and spent their money in the roads around their houses. There aren't many places left in the UK nowadays that share that kind of community spirit, but when interviewing ex-East Enders, that philosophy is still very much intrenched in their minds.

Priamo Pellicci bought the cafe from its previous owner in 1900. As well as running a successful cafe, Priamo and his wife, Elide, also brought up seven children, many of whom had a key role to play in the success of the cafe in later years. When Priamo died in 1931, Elide took over and slightly renamed the cafe E. Pellicci, which is the same name it operates under today. It was Elide who ran the cafe throughout the many years that Ronnie, Reggie and The Firm would have their breakfast there almost every morning. She was even there when Ronnie and Reggie had their first run in with the law – when Reggie was pushed by a policeman outside the cafe. When she passed away in 2008, it was taken over by Nevio Snr – who was born upstairs – and his wife Maria. Nevio and Maria were heavily involved in the day-to-day running of the cafe long before Elide gave up ownership, though. They knew the Kray twins well. In fact, in *East End Stories*, Reggie wrote:

> A memory popped into my head of sitting in Pellicci's Cafe on the Bethnal Green Road savouring a coffee and talking to good friends. Does the cafe, which has been there since the turn of the century, still open its doors every day? Does pencil-moustached Nevio Pellicci still bustle around shouting orders through to his wife Maria, or Mama as she was known? That place served the best food outside of your own mothers' kitchen and it still makes my mouth water at the thought.

## E. Pellicci's Cafe

It's their daughter, Anna, who currently owns it today. It has been awarded a Grade II Listed Status by English Heritage, fully embroidering it into both the history and the future of the East End of London. When Reggie was in prison, he even said he would do anything for one last meal at E. Pellicci.

When Ron was in prison and in and out of mental institutes, it was Reggie and his brother, Charlie, who would regularly meet in Pellicci's Cafe to discuss the Double R Club. Charlie and Reggie worked well together; there was an undertone of gangster activity, but with Ron in prison the violence had certainly died down. Like any brothers, the pair didn't always see eye to eye, but Reggie credits him with some of the more successful Kray ventures.

Charlie was never as close to Ronnie and Reggie as they were to each other, which is perhaps to be expected. Charlie's wife, Dolly, and the twins never saw eye to eye. Reggie described her as 'somebody who thought she was above the lot of us'. Dolly's distain towards the twins may have stemmed from their involvement with Barbara Windsor. It has been widely reported that Charlie and Barbara had an affair while he was married to Dolly. Eventually they broke it off and Dolly and Charlie went on to have two children.

When Double R was closed down, it was in Pellicci's that Reggie, Charlie – and Ron who was now out of prison – discussed going upmarket and getting a decent club.

At this time they were being mentored by long-time gangster Billy Hill. The Krays looked after a number of Hill's business interests and in turn he offered them advice on how to build their empire. Hill, who grew up in an established criminal family, was responsible for masterminding a number of large-scale cash robberies. He also managed to defraud London's High Society of millions. The gambling-con orchestrated by Hill was called *The Big Edge* and has been written about and researched extensively throughout history.

In short, Hill swindled some of the wealthiest people in Britain out of millions of pounds by marking cards at the Clermont Club in Mayfair's Berkeley Square. To everybody else, he was a man to avoid. To the Krays, he was an idol.

The question remains, why Pellucci's over any of the other cafes in the area? The location on Bethnal Green Road certainly helped. What's perhaps most interesting, though, is that many of my interviewees said it was where the richer working-class people went. And by 1962, Ronnie and Reggie certainly fell into that category.

# Chapter 10

# 57 Ormsby Street

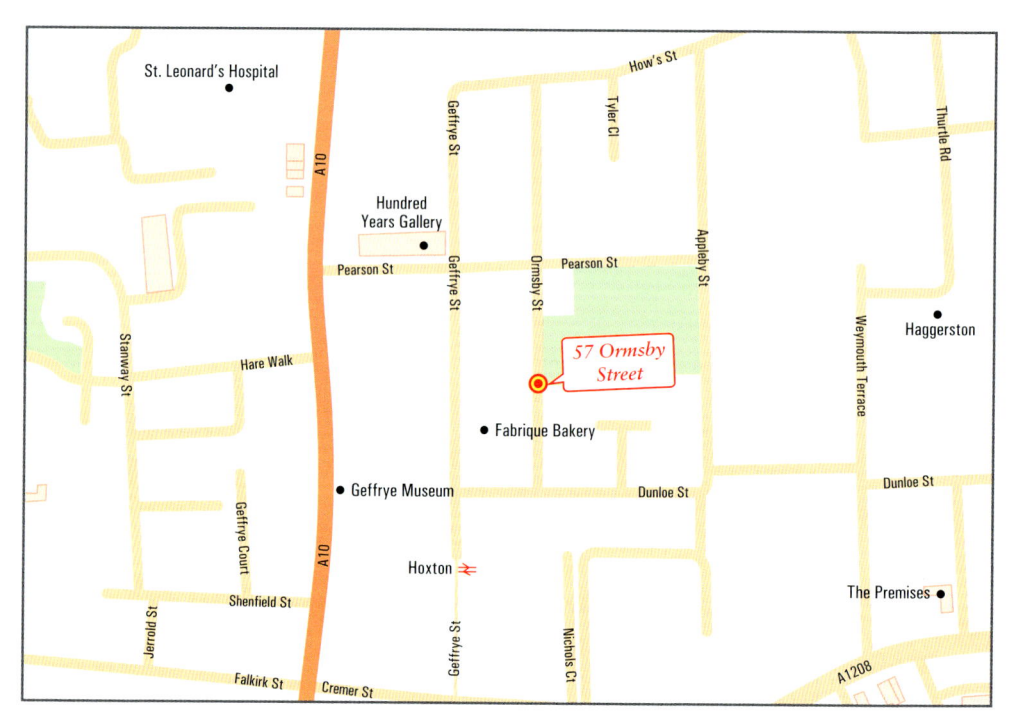

*57 Ormsby Street - Frances' family home.*

**Where?**
57 Ormsby Street
Hoxton
London
E2

**Why?**
This house belonged to Elsie and Frank Shea Snr, the parents of Frances Shea, Reggie's wife.

# 57 Ormsby Street

**How to get there:**
Ormsby Street has changed significantly since the days of Elsie and Frank, but it's a great place to visit just to experience the location in comparison to other places visited by the Kray twins around the East End of London. Ormsby Street is close to Hoxton station. If you get off at Hoxton station, walk up Geffrye Street until you reach the crossroads with Pearson Street, take a right onto Pearson Street and then when you reach the first crossroads, that's Ormsby Street. It stretches both left and right at the crossroads, but Elsie and Frank Snr lived just to the right. Their house – and even house number – no longer exists.

Before the film *Legend*, people didn't know too much about the relationship between Reggie Kray and his wife, Frances. After her portrayal in the film, she is one of the most talked about people when researching the Kray twins.

While the film honed in on the tragedy of her life, there were many nuances between the film's portrayal and her real life.

The story of Frances Shea starts in 57 Ormsby Street where she lived with her mum, dad and brother, Frank; who was a friend of Reggie's.

While Ormsby Street does still exist, there's no longer a number 57 and most of the road was completely bulldozed in the 1960s. Ormsby Street was on the same Tower Hamlets Council list as Vallance Road and was to be replaced by modern developments. This type of redevelopment happened to many areas across the East End that had survived the Blitz. As much of the East End had to be rebuilt, the council decided to bring the entirety of the East End up to date which consequently meant the end of Ormsby Street.

The humble terraced houses that lined Ormsby Street weren't an eyesore, in fact just before the road was demolished in the 1960s, it featured neat houses with identical shutters. It was undoubtedly, though, a poor area.

In *Legend*, the filming of the Shea family home took place at 32 Caradoc Street, Greenwich. This terraced street offers the viewers a close depiction of what it would have been like to walk down Ormsby Street.

Reggie first met Frances in 1962 at the door of her home after he went there to see if her brother, Frank, was available. Frank was a very minor member of The Firm, he would do odd driving jobs for them and he once sold Reggie a car. Frank and Reggie met for the first time when Reggie was looking for a different car than the Vanguard he had been driving. At the time, Frank had a car dealership in North London. He was just 18 years old when he first met Ronnie and Reggie; they struck up a friendship and he became Reggie's driver for some years.

Both he and Frances had lived at Ormsby Street their entire lives, Frank was just four years older than Frances, so they developed quite a close-knit friendship over the years. They were born to Elsie Shea, a seamstress and Frank Shea Snr, a woodworker. Originally, Elsie was from Shoreditch and Frank from Hoxton, so they were both of East End heritage, although Frank Senior did have some Irish ancestry.

Frank Shea was involved in a number of criminal dealings himself; he used to hide in the rooms of prostitutes and steal the wallets of visiting clientele. The prostitute ensured the client paid before they began and then, after their clothes had come off and had been discarded on the floor, Frank would steal their wallet and anything else he could find. The money in the wallet and other miscellaneous items would be split between him and the prostitute. At the time, his partners in crime were Chris and Tony Lambrianou, who both ended up playing middleweight roles in The Firm.

Chris Lambrianou played a particularly pivotal role in the life of The Firm and he and Frank Shea were close from their teenage days. Chris' colourful past included jail time – on more than one occasion. His first stint as a criminal – which was when he used to work with Frank and various prostitutes – saw him go to prison for two months for 'living off immoral earnings'. A number of people who knew him described him as a 'loner', but regardless of that, he had a reputation in the local area, which is what lead him to Ronnie and Reggie.

Frank wasn't in on the day that Reggie visited, but he and Frances ended up talking and Reggie asked her out. On their first date, they went to The Double R.

A pattern emerged quite quickly for them; Reggie would see Frances every night, he'd drop her back at her house and then he'd go and tour around his clubs and work.

It was behind the door of 57 Ormsby Street that the arguments started between Frances and her parents. They didn't like Reggie and her mum famously wore black on their wedding day. The idea of Frances leaving home aged 18 to marry a gangster was abhorrent to them and they made their opinions known throughout her life – and after she died.

Not many people were aware that Reggie lived at this address for a short while in between marrying Frances and moving into their own home at Cedra Court. They decided to redecorate their home before moving in, so they lived with Mr and Mrs Shea in the interim; it's not known whether the option to move into Vallance Road was available, but this gesture from Elsie and Frank Snr goes some way to show that their relationship wasn't quite as tense as the media made out in the early days of Reggie and Frances' relationship.

# Chapter 11

# The Kentucky

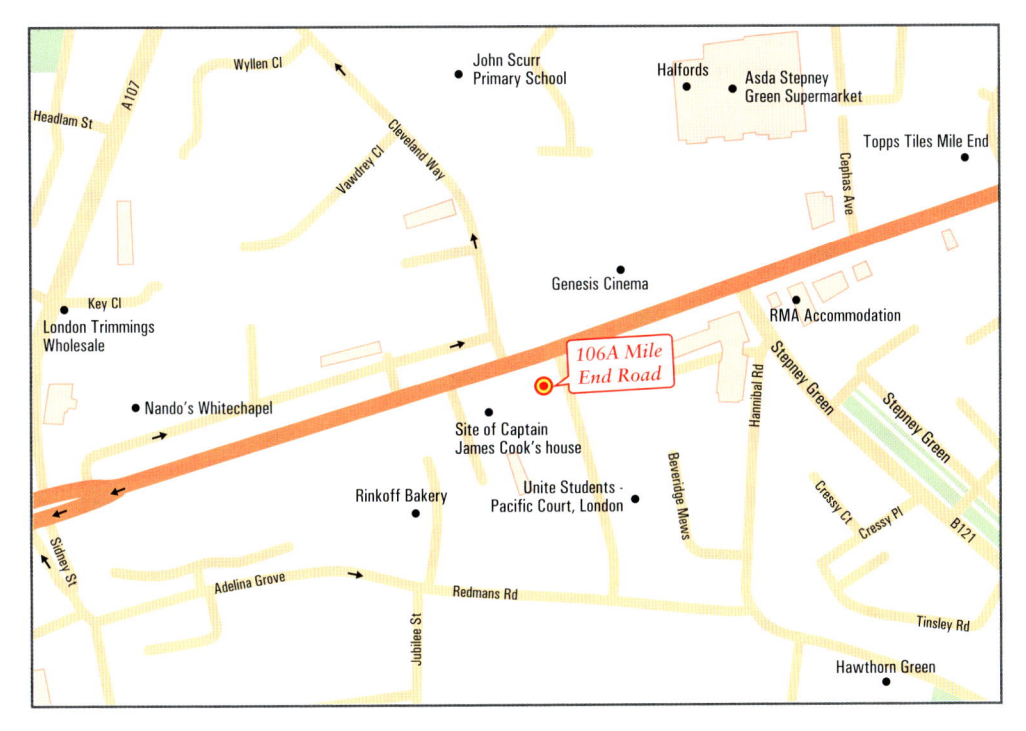

*The Kentucky, the twins' first club.*

**Where?**
106a Mile End Road
Stepney
London
E1 4UN

**Why?**
The Kentucky was Ronnie and Reggie's first upmarket club which attracted a number of celebrities, politicians and high-profile clientele.

**How to get there:**
Although The Kentucky has long since been shut down and replaced, the building still remains completely intact. It's located on Mile End Road directly between Stepney Green and Whitechapel Underground stations. Most of the key landmarks in the life of the Kray twins are around Whitechapel and Bethnal Green station, so if you get off at Whitechapel, you'll be able to see The Blind Beggar at the same time. Exit Whitechapel Underground station and turn left onto Mile End Road; it's approximately 0.3 miles from there, around a seven-minute walk. If you decide to get off at Stepney Green Underground station, simply do a right as you leave the station. You'll find the building of The Kentucky around 0.2 miles along the road – it's around a five-minute walk.

The planning undertaken by Charlie, Reggie and Ron started to pay off in the early 1960s when they opened their first up-market club: The Kentucky. Charlie had taken a backseat on this one, and the twins opened it almost entirely without his help. The pair dreamt of buying a club in the West End, but this goal was still untenable at this point. The Kentucky was the next best thing; it wasn't just any club in the East End, it was to be *the* club of the East End. It would attract custom from all across London and encourage the people of the East End to don their finery in order to gain admission.

The Kentucky was nestled in a row of beautiful Georgian houses. The original building is still there to this day and is now a grill restaurant, though it has changed hands on many occasions since The Kentucky. The Georgian townhouses in London are some of the most beautifully designed houses anywhere. They often appear on the glossy pages of interiors magazines, their sash windows and panelled doors a telltale sign of classic, British design.

In the past, the building underwent a large-scale renovation to retain some of the period features it now possesses. There was a time – around 2008 – where the two buildings flanking the property looked far superior to the building that used to house The Kentucky. At the time, the building's signature brickwork had been completely covered with a layer of grey cement and the sash windows had been replaced with nondescript PVC double-glazing. Renovated to its former glory, you can now tell that this building underwent renovation works more recently than the rest of its counterparts. Its new drainage system, grey sash windows and slightly lighter brick colour way are key signs of new-age townhouse restorations.

When Ronnie and Reggie purchased the property, the pair spent £2,000 on the upholstery. This might not seem like a lot today, but taking inflation into consideration, this is the equivalent of spending around £40,000 in 2019. That's a lot of money for most people, but it's especially a lot of money for two people who were living in one of the poorest areas of the UK. They funded this new business venture with the money from their previously successful ventures; The Regal and The Double R Club, they also paid for some of it with the ever-increasing pot of money they were making from the protection racket.

The club was a triumph; it had a black leather and glass bar, red walls and a four-foot high stage big enough to accommodate a five-piece band. Each table was dimly lit

## The Kentucky

with a small lamp and there was an intimate dance floor in front of the stage. In many ways, it emulated the look of the Double R, but this time it was attracting even more high-profile clientele.

Barbara Windsor – a good friend of the twins – asked Reggie if they could film some of the scenes of *Sparrows Can't Sing* there. He agreed. At the time, although Barbara Windsor had been in a handful of films, it was still quite an early point in her career. The *Carry On* films, which started – for her – with *Carry On Spying*, didn't come out until 1964. *Sparrows Can't Sing* came out in 1963 so at this point she was teetering on the edge of worldwide fame.

Throughout their lives, Barbara Windsor remained very close to the Kray twins. She admitted in her autobiography, *All Of Me*, that she had a one-night stand with Reggie Kray while she was married to Ronnie Knight – another East End gangster. She also had a longer affair with the twins' brother, Charlie while he was married.

The film's premiere was held in the Empire Cinema opposite the club and many of the cast and crew went back to The Kentucky for the afterparty. Attendees included the likes of Lord Snowden and Roger Moore. Princess Margaret was also in attendance at the premiere, but decided not to go to the after party at The Kentucky. The Krays had infiltrated the celebrity world and were now making headway in the political world. They never, however, managed to rub shoulders with royalty and they did try on quite a few occasions.

The evening drew in much press and business was booming. Countless celebrities graced the dance floor of The Kentucky that night and were more than happy to gush about their experience to the media. This encouraged yet more customers through the doors, they weren't just locals, either; news had spread into West London and The Kentucky became something of a hotspot across the whole of London.

Ron came into his own at The Kentucky Club. Seeing himself as an entertainment manager of sorts, he was the one who booked appearances at the club, many of which were deemed highly successful. Once again, Tex The Dwarf was back, but the guests at The Kentucky Club took to the act a lot better than those at The Double R had. Both regulars and one-time customers alike would talk enthusiastically about the type of acts that came into the club. At the time, no other club in the East End of London was offering such a variety of performances with the added benefit of an upmarket feel. People liked being able to dress up in their finest outfits and rub shoulders with celebrities and high-profile individuals. East Enders were just as welcome as those from the West End and it became an everyman club, attracting a whole range of different personalities.

After an exciting couple of years, the club was closed in 1964. The police didn't like the idea of the twins having a license and took their objections to Stepney Borough Council. The police reported that the pair were running the club badly – which included illegal drinking and gambling. The twins vehemently opposed this, claiming there were no illegal activities going on at The Kentucky. At this point, though, the Krays already had a reputation, so it's understandable why Stepney Borough Council decided not to give Ronnie and Reggie the benefit of the doubt.

This, in turn, led the pair back to focusing all of their efforts into protection money. At this point, they were getting most of their money from protecting local businesses. They weren't precious about what type of businesses they protected, and perhaps one of the most controversial of their clientele was Peter Rachman.

Rachman was a Polish-born landlord who became famous around the Notting Hill area of London during the 1950s and '60s for the exploitation of his tenants. The word 'Rachmanism' even entered the Oxford English Dictionary as a word for exploitation and intimidation of tenants. It has been widely reported that Peter Rachman had no shame when it came to how he behaved towards his tenants. He would often split large properties up into small rooms specifically to appeal to prostitutes and immigrants, many of whom had little knowledge about their rights and the laws that governed the renting market. He was described as a 'slum landlord' and was also prosecuted twice for brothel-keeping.

Peter Rachman made the mistake of not paying the Kray twins for their protection efforts and he had a lot of people after him at that point. It came to a head in 1960 in Esmeralda's Barn, which also became the setting of their next business venture.

# Chapter 12

# Wandsworth Prison

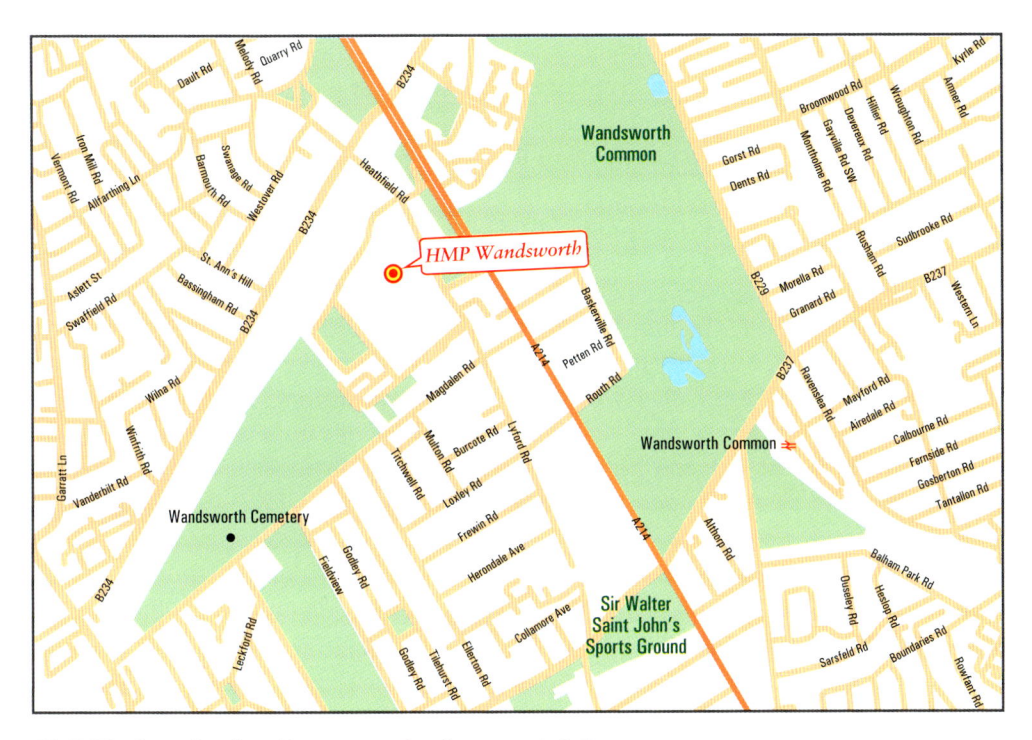

*HMP Wandsworth; where Reggie spent his first spate in jail.*

## Where?
HM Wandsworth Prison
Heathfield Road
London
SW18 3HU

## Why?
Both Ronnie and Reggie served time behind bars at HM Wandsworth Prison, where they also met some pivotal characters; two of whom would impact their futures in a big way.

**How to get there:**
Wandsworth Prison isn't particularly close by to any of the other Kray landmarks dotted around the East End, but it's an interesting place to visit nonetheless, particularly because there's some beautiful parks and other landmarks in the area. Wandsworth Common station is the nearest to the prison and the journey from the station to the prison is quite a nice one, which involves walking through Wandsworth Common. In total, it's a fifteen minute walk (0.8 miles). Leave the station and head towards Wandsworth Common. Enter the park opposite The Hope Pub and take the main path into the park. The path will bring you out onto Trinity Road. Keep walking until you reach the County Arms Pub. Take a left as you walk past it and walk alongside the pub onto Alma Terrace. At this point, you will see the outline of the prison at the end of the road. The entrance to the front of the prison is just to the right as you walk out onto Heathfield Road. The entrance is perhaps the grandest part of the building and certainly worth a look; it retains many of its original features.

Wandsworth Prison is one of the largest prisons in Western Europe, homing 1,628 prisoners. Built in 1851, much of the building is still intact and little has changed from when Reggie and Ronnie were inmates.

Other notable inmates include Ronnie Biggs, who escaped the prison while serving a thirty-year sentence for his part in the Great Train Robbery. As well as Ronnie Biggs, Rolf Harris, Pete Doherty, Oscar Wilde, Max Clifford, Julian Assange and Gary Glitter have all served time here. That might seem like quite a few famous faces for one prison, but its size and location means it was an obvious choice of prison for people who were local to London and sentenced at the Old Bailey.

It was also the site of 135 executions between 1878 and 1961. One of the people executed, for murder, was Francis Forsyth. He was one of only four 18-year-olds executed in a British prison in the twentieth century. The gallows where the 135 people were executed were kept in full working order until 1994 when it was made into a tea room.

In 1964, as the relationship between Reggie and Frances was progressing, Reggie was sentenced to six months in Wandsworth Prison, a category B men's prison. It was during this time that the majority of the love letters sent between Reggie and Frances were written. In recent years, many of these letters have found their way into the hands of the media and they make for quite an interesting read. Snippets like:

> I am sorry you are in prison. Don't worry. When you come out I'll make your favourite toast and marmalade for your breakfast. I love you. Please remember me.

Sent from Frances, highlighted their close bond and also the simplicity of their lives together in relation to Reggie's complex criminal life. Reggie's time in Wandsworth Prison was the final straw for Frances' parents, though, who already had a fraught relationship with their soon-to-be son-in-law. Reggie proposed a while after he was released from prison, without her parents' permission.

## Wandsworth Prison

Both Reggie and Ronnie spent time in Wandsworth Prison. Ronnie was sentenced to three years in 1956 and Reggie to six months in 1962.

Reggie was arrested when he went to visit a shop owner who was withholding his protection money from them. When he arrived and began speaking to the shop owner, he found that the police were hiding in the next room and listening to his whole conversation. He was quickly sentenced to six months.

The time Ronnie spent in jail coincided with Reggie's success with The Double R. Ronnie was sentenced to three years at Wandsworth Prison after his involvement with a West End drinking club called The Stragglers just off of Cambridge Circus. The owner, a man called Billy Jones, was overwhelmed by the amount of fights taking place at the club; various gangs were demanding protection money from him and every time the club security guards removed any gang member from the club, they would come back and destroy it. It was a costly and never-ending battle for Jones.

He enlisted the help of Ronnie and Reggie. There was a noticeable difference from the offset and many of the low-level criminals decided it wasn't worth getting on the wrong side of the Kray twins. With the amount of trouble brewing, though, it was just a matter of time before a gang struck again. Eventually, a gang of Irish dockers called the Watney Streeters beat up a partner of Billy's named Bobby Ramsey.

At this point, the gangs were at loggerheads with each other. It wasn't an option for Ronnie and Reggie to simply leave the Watney Streeters, it was a matter of pride for them; they had to retaliate. Reggie wasn't involved in the second battle with the Watney Streeters; Ronnie, Billy and Bobby struck while they were at a local pub. One particular gang member, Jackie Martin, got very badly hurt. The East End underworld had an unspoken code of conduct whereby they didn't name and shame the gang members involved in hurting them. Jackie Martin shared no such code of conduct and he readily named Ronnie, Billy and Bobby. Thus began Ronnie's three years in Wandsworth Prison.

It was during this stint that Ronnie met two pivotal characters. He wouldn't have known it at the time, but Frank Mitchell and Jack McVitie played a critical role in the lives of both Ronnie and Reggie. Reggie got to know Frank Mitchell particularly well because of how close he and Ronnie were in prison, and due to Reggie's regular visits.

Although this was Ronnie's first time in a men's prison, Frank Mitchell was a seasoned prisoner. He was just 19 years old when he went to prison for the first time, this was shortly followed by another stint in 1952. He was known for his ability to escape from any prison and Ronnie – and Reggie when he came to visit – both warmed to him.

Jack McVitie arrived at Wandsworth Prison towards the end of Ronnie's sentence. He had been sentenced to seven years' imprisonment for being in possession of explosives and possessing a flick-knife. Jack McVitie wanted to work for The Firm after meeting Ronnie in prison – and as an extension of that, he had also met Reggie. In the first instance, when Jack was released from prison, Ronnie and Reggie reluctantly allowed him to do odd jobs for them. Jack McVitie had quite a violent side to him – which was highlighted during his ever-frequent drunken spells.

Wandsworth Prison was eight miles away from Vallance Road, but the family were very involved in going to visit the men while they were in jail. When Ronnie was in prison, Reggie and Violet would make regular visits, and while Reggie was in prison Ronnie, Frances and Violet would visit.

# Chapter 13

# Esmeralda's Barn

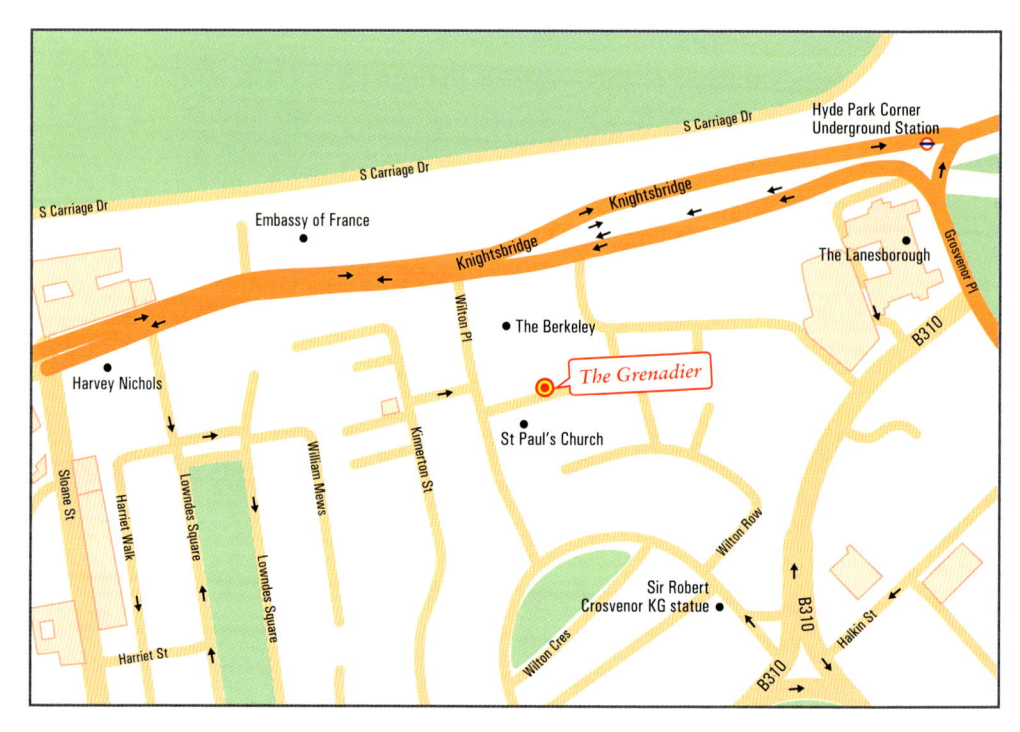

*Esmeralda's Barn; the established West End club that the twins acquired.*

**Where:**
Wilton Place
Knightsbridge
London
SW1X 7RL

**Why:**
This was the Kray twins' first West End club and there was some controversy over how they came to acquire it.

## *Esmeralda's Barn*

**How to get there:**
Esmeralda's Barn used to sit where the five-star hotel, The Berkeley, now stands. The best underground station to get off at is Knightsbridge. Leave the tube station and head right, Hyde Park should be on your left as you walk along. After about three minutes, you will see Wilton Place on your right. Almost immediately as you enter Wilton Place, you'll notice The Berkeley directly across the road. As you can see, this is quite prime real estate and it was much the same when the Krays acquired it.

To set up the story of Esmeralda's Barn, it's first important to realise the opulence of this setting in comparison to both the Double R Club and The Kentucky Club. This was an established West End club, with close proximity to Hyde Park and the high-end shops around Knightsbridge; this location was exactly what the pair were looking for.

There are two stories of how Ronnie and Reggie came to acquire this club. In all interviews with the pair, they've been illusive about the subject. It is a fact that the Krays had dealings with Peter Rachman around the same time they acquired Esmeralda's Barn, but the two stories offer a different sequence of events.

The first involves Peter Rachman, who began acquiring a large number of buildings around this time. At his peak, it was said that he built up an empire that consisted of hundreds of mansion blocks and several nightclubs.

When Rachman kept avoiding paying his protection money to the Krays, Ronnie met him at Esmeralda's Barn, which at this point was owned by Stefan de Faye. The club was a legitimate gambling club and, although de Faye had his own colourful past, it seemed that he played by the rules as far as the club was concerned; he didn't allow gambling in his club until it was legalised in the Betting and Gaming Act 1960. However, this was almost irrelevant because the club wasn't making any money. Both de Faye and his partner Mr Burns couldn't decide on what the club should be and so it plateaued.

In Esmeralda's Barn, Rachman gave Ronnie a cheque to clear his debts, but the cheque bounced. At this point, Rachman was nowhere to be found. Although he had a lot of abhorrent qualities, Rachman was a clever man; he knew that once he started paying the Krays for protection, they'd demand more and more.

One of the stories, therefore, claims that Rachman arranged for Ronnie and Reggie to buy Esmeralda's Barn for £1,000. He did this through Leslie Payne, Ronnie's financial advisor, because he didn't want to meet them face to face given their current situation. Payne was already deeply involved with the Kray twins, but at this point he had been given the unofficial title of Ron's financial advisor. To sum up their relationship, Leslie would use his experience in fraudulent activities of the past. All the while, Payne stayed one step removed from the violent side of Ronnie and Reggie's business; it was out of his comfort zone, he was purely more of a numbers man.

Between the pair, they arranged the sale, convincing Stefan de Faye that he was out of his depth in a club industry that – at the time – was largely operated by gangsters.

De Faye himself was no stranger to criminal activity; he became involved in some long-term frauds; he'd buy goods on credit, sell them on as quickly as he could and then disappear before he could be caught by the credit companies. As a result, he'd already had brief dealings with the twins.

This – the story of the Kray twins hustling Stefan de Faye out of his club with the help of Peter Rachman – is one version of events. In Charlie Kray's book *Doing The Business – The Final Confession Of The Senior Kray Brother*, Charlie offers up a different take on it.

Charlie found out about the club through Commander Diamond – a gentleman of means who was well known to everybody in the West End of London. He regularly rubbed shoulders with London's aristocracy and celebrities and had connections everywhere.

Commander Diamond, who was an old friend of Charlie's, had realised – having seen how much Stefan de Faye was struggling – that Esmeralda's Barn was a fine opportunity for somebody with experience. As he knew the area well and lived just around the corner, Commander Diamond was able to give quite a detailed assessment of where the problems lay. It was also in his best interest to have the Krays close by; it offered him an extra level of protection.

Charlie then got Leslie Payne, Ron's business manager, involved and they met at Commander Diamond's Knightsbridge flat along with Freddie Gore, their accountant. Freddie Gore stayed largely under the radar but he certainly knew what was going on behind the scenes of the Krays' expanding empire.

As well as Charlie, Leslie and Freddie, Commander Diamond invited Stefan de Faye and Mr Burns. As soon as the meeting got under way, de Faye felt he was being ambushed, he also felt that Charlie Kray and his brothers had no business being in the West End of London. Charlie – who was quite level-headed throughout this exchange – was certainly angered by the mention of his East End roots. The Kray family did not like to be told where they could and could not do business.

As awkwardness descended on the room, Charlie decided to tell the men the story of his life so far and the hardship his parents had faced raising children in a poor part of London. They were a captivated crowd. Charlie finished the story by saying that they'd offer the pair £2,000 for the club and that if they didn't take it, the club would be taken off of them anyway. Charlie left there with a deal to take over Esmeralda's Barn for £2,000.

The stories are both quite similar, but one involves Charlie Kray and Commander Diamond and the other involves Peter Rachman. Both are widely publicised, but whichever version of events is true, Esmeralda's Barn changed hands and belonged to Ronnie and Reggie.

Lord Effingham was paid £10 per week to serve on the board of directors. Ronnie and Reggie tried to do everything right; as well as having Lord Effingham on the board, they took on experienced staff to help run it.

In trying to do everything correctly, this quickly turned into the first club that Ronnie and Reggie didn't run well. They accrued a large amount of debt in a short space of time. Although the club was successful, bringing in the likes of Lucien Freud and Francis Bacon, the amount the twins were paying out in order to keep the club afloat was outweighing what they were bringing in.

They paid the staff a lot; Ronnie was able to choose the waiters and croupiers and regularly made poor decisions based on the level of attractiveness of the men he employed rather than their expertise. Ronnie let his personal life intertwine with the business and Esmeralda's Barn became the setting for a lot of Ronnie's vices. Much like Double R, it was Ronnie who discouraged visitors.

Reggie had his part to play in the demise of Esmeralda's Barn too, though. With his new celebrity gangster status, Reggie would regularly waiver the bar tabs and bills from other gangsters and celebrities in the community. Even when they didn't waiver the bills regularly, the celebrities and aristocracy that the Barn attracted would just decide not to pay. It was significantly harder for the Kray twins to use their bullish tactics with this type of clientele.

It wasn't the police that had something to say about this particular Kray twins' venture, though, it was the Inland Revenue. Their accountant, Freddie Gore, hadn't been paying taxes correctly – if at all – and Ronnie and Reggie were dealt an ultimatum: go to prison or pay your bills. They picked the latter and left the West End with their tails between their legs.

# Chapter 14

# The Hideaway/El Morocco

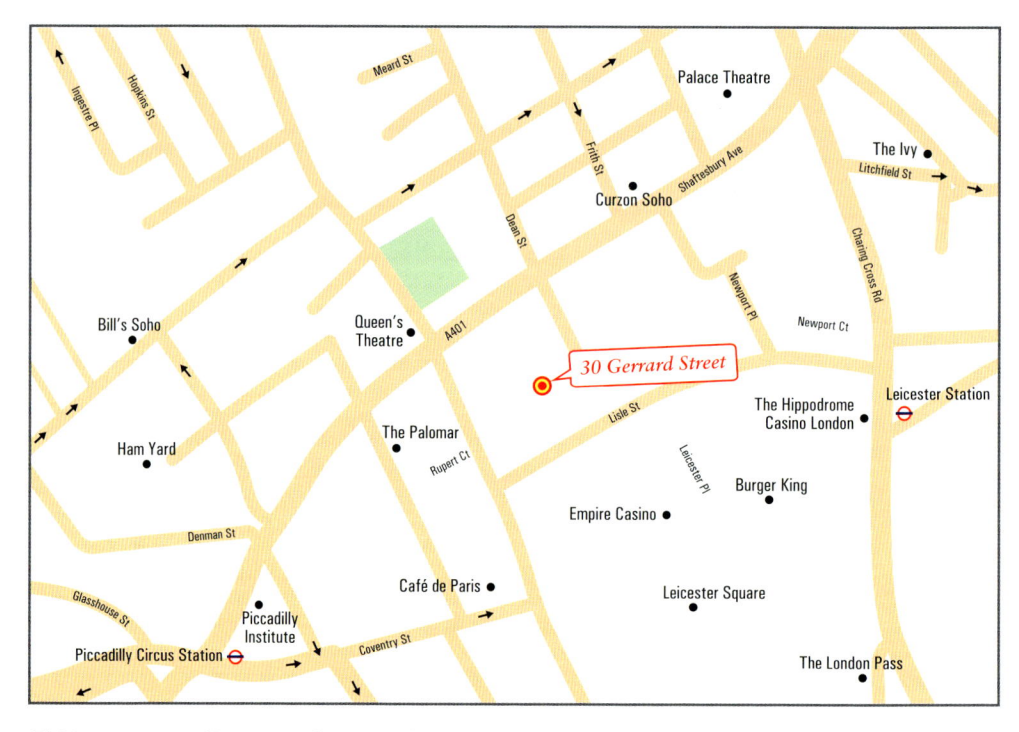

*El Morocco, one of Ronnie and Reggie's last successful endeavours.*

**Where?**
30 Gerrard Street
Westminster
London
W1D 6JS

**Why?**
El Morocco was the pinnacle in the Kray twins' success. It was around this time that Ronnie and Reggie were at the very top of the East End gangsters' hall of fame.

## The Hideaway/El Morocco

**How to get there:**
Gerrard Street is in the very centre of London and is now more famously known as Chinatown. You can get off at Leicester Square Underground station and head onto Charing Cross Road. Head right past Angus Steakhouse and take the first left onto Little Newport Street, then take the first left onto Newport Place. As you're walking, you'll notice the entrance to Chinatown on your left. 30 Gerrard Street is nearer the other end of the street.

Many people I've interviewed had differing opinions on the Kray twins, but it's largely thought that a factor in their notoriety was that they never gave up. The Hideaway was a testament to that theory.

Shortly after the closure of Esmeralda's Barn, the twin's next opportunity presented itself. 30 Gerrard Street is now right in the centre of Chinatown, a popular tourist hotspot in central London. The club itself is now a Chinese restaurant, but the building is still the same, so – in the hustle of Chinatown, it's surprisingly quite possible to get a sense of the grandeur of the club by standing outside 30 Gerrard Street.

The twins went for a particular style of building and architecture. Similar to The Kentucky, the building had a Georgian Townhouse feel to it. The large paned windows and light brickwork were reminiscent of their previous venture. The only notable difference was the location; this one was located right in the centre of London. Although Gerrard Street wasn't quite as busy as it is now, the club had a significant footfall from the offset. This, teamed with the gentleman's club feel that the building exuded, made it a worthy investment.

In 1964, The Hideaway nightclub was bought by Hew McCowan; at the time it was operating under the name Bon Soir. Hew McCowan was a baronet's son and a socialite by all accounts, who planned to turn the Soho nightclub into a fashionable spot for his upmarket friends. Unlike many of the other hotspots Ronnie and Reggie had previously been involved in, this particular venture was unlikely to need protecting. Its prime location and Hew McCowan's socialite groups of friends meant that it wasn't the type of place to attract unsavoury characters. Nonetheless, they wanted to place themselves back in the heart of the West End scene, so they saw this as an opportunity to negotiate with McCowan.

He offered them 20 per cent of his new venture, but then changed his mind. It's not known the exact reason for this change of heart, but it would've only taken a bit of light research on Hew McCowan's part for him to discover the Kray twins' colourful past.

The pair did not take this well; they saw this as an act of hostility and went to the club to demand money. This type of intimidation and bullish behaviour, though, was not as well received in the West End of London. Although the Krays had a following that spanned far wider than London by this point, their clout was primarily within the underworld and through criminal networks. Hew McCowan, therefore, wasn't intimidated by this.

Up until this point, business owners in the East End rarely, if ever, told the police about the Krays' dealings. The twins had more clients in the East End – from whom they were still extorting protection money – but they also had some smaller businesses in the West End. Most of the businesses they worked with in the West End tended to be involved in unsavoury activities of one type or another and needed the safety that the Krays' protection could offer them. Hew McCowan didn't subscribe to this mentality, though, and went straight to the police.

After trying and failing to offer a bail amount of £18,000, three trials and fifty-six days remanded in custody, the twins were found not guilty. They were originally arrested on a charge of demanding money with menaces in connection to the protection racket they had been running. Hew McCowan claimed that the twins had asked for a stake in the business in return for them supplying two doormen to 'protect' the club. The twins denied this charge and said that there was no mention of them ever providing protection in return for a stake in the club.

When the trial eventually came to an end, the jury couldn't reach a decision. As a result, a retrial was ordered which ended in the brothers' acquittal.

They went on to buy the club and changed its name to El Morocco. It's still not clear how they were able to make this happen, but some locals believed that Hew McCowan failed to rouse local interest in his upmarket club and so took a step back.

The not-guilty verdict was one a number of people were dubious of. Many believe the twins used their connections with Lord Boothby, the British politician, to smooth the matter over with the Old Bailey. Whenever a witness came forward, they'd quickly change their story or withdraw their claims. There is no doubt that Lord Boothby's involvement had an impact on the verdict; the jury gave their verdict after ten minutes: not guilty. A verdict which came a little while after Lord Boothby had asked a question on behalf of the Krays in the House Of Lords.

The Krays had a skill of selecting the right friends-in-high-places throughout their lives. They were never short of high-profile and celebrity friends. In many cases, it was the Krays' celebrity status that launched careers; the singer, David Essex, is an example of this.

The name El Morocco came from Ron's love of Tangiers; he'd visited Morocco on holiday in the previous year. He was particularly enamoured by the place and had a keen eye for interiors. Everybody commented on how his flat had a middle-eastern vibe to it. Although Reggie had decorated each club the pair owned, this one had a distinctively different feel to it. It wasn't quite the plush, mirror-adorned, dancefloor-centric clubs of years gone by. El Morocco was more of a themed experience and no stone was left unturned in Ronnie's bid to offer an immersive Moroccan experience to each guest through the doors.

David Essex, the London-born singer and performer, was one of the first entertainers Ronnie and Reggie signed up to have a regular spot at El Morocco. This was one of his first ever regular gigs; at the time, he was relatively unknown. Years later, when Reggie was in Parkhurst, he saw David Essex send his greetings to Charlie, Ronnie and Reggie on TV.

*The Hideaway/El Morocco*

1965, by all accounts, was a good year for the Kray twins. Their businesses had finally settled down and were providing a steady income stream, Ron's mental health was up and down, but wasn't at its worst, and Reggie married Frances Shea.

Ronnie and Reggie were making a large amount of money from protection, they had a monopoly over Soho and the West End. Clubs under their protection included the Gigi and the New Life in Firth Street, the New Mill off Shaftesbury Avenue, the Bagatelle off Regent Street and the Starlight off Oxford Street.

Everything was seemingly running smoothly. The year to come, though, proved to be the most challenging yet for the Kray twins.

# Chapter 15

# St James The Great Church

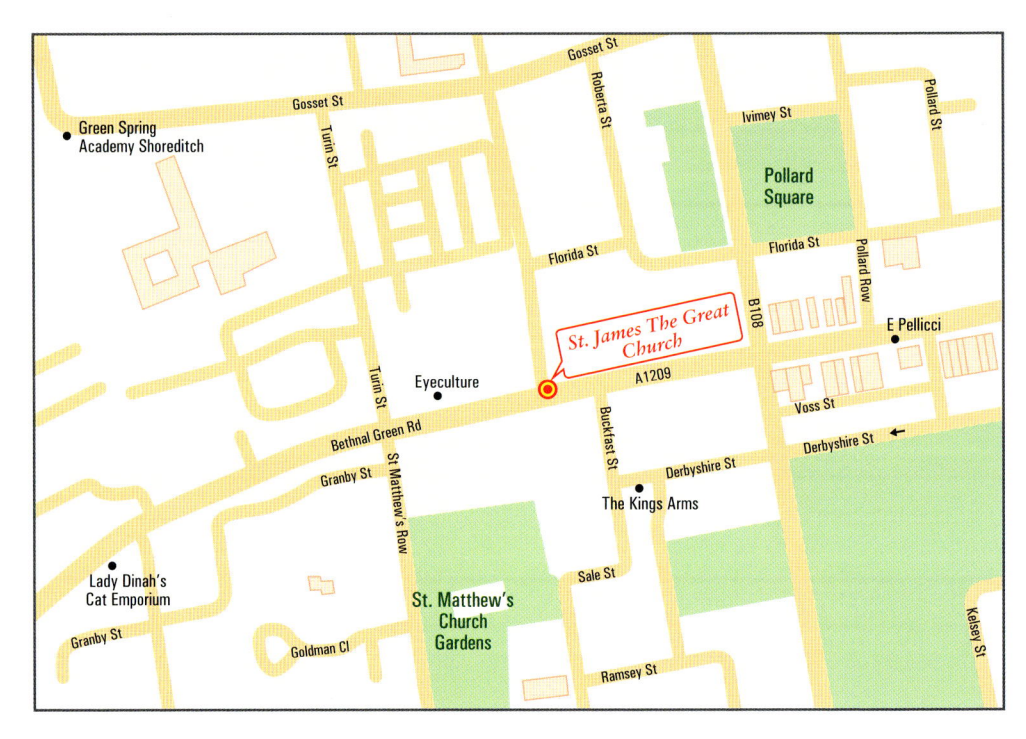

*St James The Great Church where Reggie and Frances got married in 1965.*

**Where?**
St James The Great Church
326 Bethnal Green Road
Bethnal Green
London
E2 0AG

**Why?**
This beautifully designed church was where Reggie Kray was married to Frances Shea on 19 April 1965.

## *St James The Great Church*

**How to get there:**
As well as many other haunts of the Kray twins, St James The Great Church can be found on Bethnal Green Road, directly opposite to E. Pellicci. From Bethnal Green Underground station, it's a short walk along Bethnal Green Road to reach the church. It can be found on the right-hand side of the road. It's also just as simple to get off at Shoreditch High Street station and walk along Bethnal Green Road from there. The walk is a little longer from Shoreditch High Street station but there are a number of interesting stops along the way.

The beautiful red-brick church on Bethnal Green Road was where Reggie and Frances got married on 19 April 1965. The church was a stone's throw away from a number of the Krays' regular haunts: Vallance Road, E. Pellicci's Cafe and Cheshire Street, putting it in easy reach for many of their East End guests.

The church still looks exactly as it did on the day of their wedding, except it has been converted into apartments. The frontage of the building has still been kept largely intact, though. It was once described as the 'Red Church' – the name needs no explanation. The stunning red brick interspersed with flashes of bright white around the window panes is quite a spectacle.

It stands out among the other buildings in the road, most of which are quite ordinary in comparison.

The church was built by master architect, Edward Blore, who worked on the expansion of Buckingham Palace and the restoration of Lambeth Palace, as well as working on Westminster Abbey and St James' Palace. The construction took place between 1840 and 1844. It's a classic example of Victorian architecture and when making comparisons, it's evident that the likes of St Pancras railway station was built at the same sort of time as Edward Blore's masterpiece.

The Victorian period of architecture was the first period in which Middle Eastern and Asian influences became apparent. There is something about the shapes and number of windows dotted around St James The Great Church that provides a nod to Middle Eastern influences.

Edward Blore didn't just stick to what was in 'fashion' architecturally, though, and that's perhaps why he was so popular in his time. Instead, for this particular building, he merged the popular red brick style of the Gothic Revival with the towering turrets of the Renaissance Revival. Although both types of architectures were very popular in Victorian times, it's important to note Edward Blore's striking ability to merge two styles – and possibly even more, to the eagle eye – with such elegance.

It has also been suggested that Edward Blore's work could be described as English Gothic, or more commonly, 'Early English Style'. This style originated in France and can be categorised by the inclusion of pointed arches, vaulted roofs, large windows and spires; all of which can be found at St James The Great Church.

When it opened in 1844, the Reverend Edward Coke made the church the first in London where poorer couples across the city could get married for free. As a result, young couples would turn up to the church in batches. This was seen as a great way to engage the local people with the church. Although attendance was a lot higher then than it is now, Edward Coke believed he had somewhat of a challenge on his hands to include both the younger and the poorer communities into church life. As well as this initiative, he raised a large amount of funding for the church and founded a dispensary, a visiting society and a Sunday School.

The church was lucky to survive as much of the surrounding area had been bombed during the Second World War, or closed for post-war redevelopment. Bethnal Green Road, in particular, was seen as a key area of redevelopment. It was most likely the unique beauty of the church and its resolute structure which saved it from demolition in the 1960s. It closed in 1987 and in 2017, one of the apartments located within the old church building was put up for sale for £365,000.

Two hundred guests were invited to what was the East End's wedding of the year between Reggie and Frances. Many of the locals saw it as the marriage of East End royalty and a large number of people showed up, invited or not, to witness the day.

In his only assignment *ever* as a wedding photographer, David Bailey captured the day. David Bailey had a unique relationship with the Kray twins, which he looked upon with fondness in many of his interviews. Describing the East End in an interview with *The Guardian* he said: 'You have to understand people ate tea leaves they were so poor. They'd do anything to feed their children. It's time and place, easy to judge, easy to be pompous.'

He went on to describe the Kray twins as Tolstoy's *Cossacks*; anarchists with their own morality. He was vocal about his fondness for Reggie – even though he slashed David Bailey's father's face with a razor – and described Ronnie as a basket of rattlesnakes. Reggie confided in David about his career and his admiration for David's ability to make a success of himself in a straight-up way.

Their relationship – although widely publicised – wasn't a friendship as such, it was more of a business relationship. It wasn't just Reggie's wedding that David photographed either, he also worked with Ronnie, Reggie and Charlie on a range of portraits, many of which are the most shared of the Kray imagery.

Other well-known guests at Reggie and Frances' wedding included boxers, Terry Allen, Terry Spinks, Ted 'Kid' Lewis and the Clark Brothers. Frances wouldn't have known many of the people invited, a lot of whom were business associates of Reggie's, but she certainly commanded the room in the imagery that was released after the wedding had taken place.

The reception took place in the Finsbury Park Hotel and they were driven to the hotel in a maroon Rolls-Royce while onlookers and wedding guests cheered them off.

By all accounts – apart from perhaps those of Frances' family, who were still struggling to come to terms with their marriage, the day was a success. The pair left the reception early and went straight to Athens for their honeymoon.

# Chapter 16

# Cedra Court

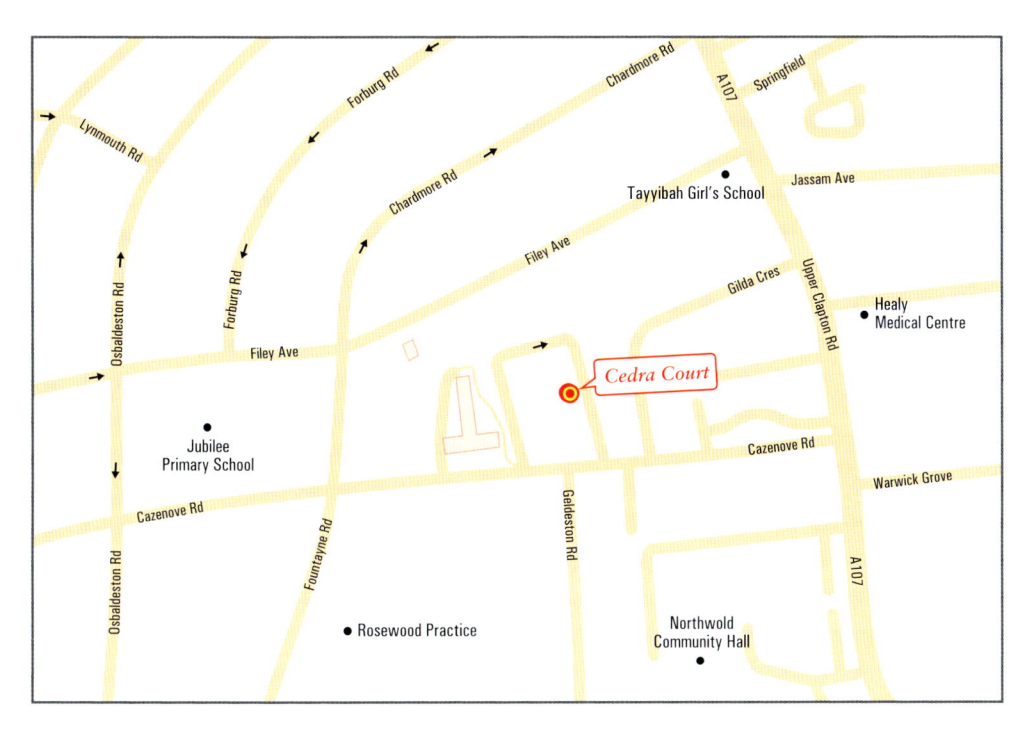

*Cedra Court; where Reggie and Frances lived in flat 1, and Ronnie in flat 8.*

**Where?**
Flat 1 and Flat 8
Cedra Court
Cazenove Road
London
N16 6AT

**Why?**
Both Ronnie and Reggie lived in these flats in the 1960s. Ronnie lived in flat 8 and Reggie and Frances lived in flat 1.

**How to get there:**
Cedra Court is not near Bethnal Green and many of the other areas of interest, but it's certainly worth a visit. It's also close to Evering Road, which is another area of interest. It's a nine-minute (0.5 mile) walk from Clapton station. Leave the station and turn left onto the A107. Pass Evering Road on the left and keep walking until you reach Cazenove Road on the left. Walk a short distance down the road until you see Cedra Court on your right.

Cedra Court is perhaps one of the most poignant places to visit. Not only is the block of flats where both Ronnie and Reggie lived still standing, it looks almost identical to how it looked when they lived there. Visiting Cedra Court feels like stepping back in time; knowing so much about what happened in flat 1 and flat 8 can almost evoke a sense of nostalgia for a time many of us never actually witnessed.

The flats were built at the beginning of the 1960s and they ooze art-deco style. Each flat looks over onto a communal garden and a select few have balconies. At the time, this type of building was springing up all across London. Much of the residential areas built around London at the time had this style. Nowadays it can be considered quite dated, but then it was the epitome of elegance. Large portions of London had been demolished post-war because of the damage inflicted on them and this large-scale demolition made way for a new era of housing architecture to erupt.

The mark of an art-deco inspired house is the blocky frontage. Quite often, each block will be arranged in a geometric fashion. Blocks that jutted out from the front of houses and flats often had curved edges to soften the building. This era in architecture was very short lived, which is why we don't see many buildings of this kind today.

The residents of Cedra Court have noticed a rise in people visiting this modest road since the film *Legend*, but it has been a popular spot for people interested in the duo long before then. The film includes Cedra Court in multiple scenes because it's so similar to how it was in the 1960s, making it the perfect, true-to-life backdrop. There are a handful of sites available to view that still look the same or very similar to how they looked when The Krays were here, but this is the one that resonates most.

Ronnie moved to Cedra Court first in the summer of 1962. They had just bought The Kentucky after his time in jail. He rented flat number 8 in Leslie Payne's name. We met Leslie Payne earlier on in the book and know his relationship with Ronnie was very up and down. 'Up and down' could also be used to describe a number of Ronnie's business relationships. It wasn't uncommon for him to wholeheartedly hang on the words of a member of The Firm for one minute, and then be plotting to have them killed the next. Leslie Payne was no exception, but at the time of Ronnie's move into Cedra Court, they were close and he respected Leslie's opinion.

Aged 29, this was Ron's first time living away from Vallance Road. It was four miles away and out of the radius of all the other ventures in his life. He was not to be without his brother for long, though; Reggie moved into flat 1 with his wife Frances a year later in the summer of 1963. This happened around the same time that Esmeralda's Barn closed.

## Cedra Court

Flat 1 was directly below flat 8, but the decor was very different. While Reggie's taste was more muted, Ron's told a story of his holidays in Tangiers and supposedly his bedroom was dwarfed by a large four-poster bed and floor-to-ceiling mirrors. Much like the themed feel of El Morocco, Ronnie's home followed a similar pattern.

Cedra Court is the central hub for a lot of question marks that still hang over Ronnie and Reggie's heads. It is believed that Ronnie's flat was the meeting point for a number of arranged orgies. The orgies were arranged by Ronnie on behalf of Lord Boothby.

Ronnie's relationship was Lord Boothby was one that the media examined time and time again. Boothby was openly bisexual in a time when homosexuality was a criminal offence. He had many affairs throughout his younger years and particularly while studying at Oxford. It's alleged that they were introduced by East End cat burglar, Leslie Holt, after he and Lord Boothby began having an affair. It is believed that the role Ronnie played in their friendship was to supply Boothby with a string of young men in return for favours of a personal matter, including campaigning for the twins in the House of Lords. This association eventually became too embarrassing for Lord Boothby, who, at this point, was described as a 'disgraced Labour MP'.

At the time, though, it's believed their relationship was strictly a business arrangement and Ronnie would host Lord Boothby at his house with a selection of male companions. In return, Boothby would stick up for Ronnie's best interests.

As a result of some of the speculation about the pair, the *Sunday Mirror* and the *Daily Mirror* had to pay Lord Boothby £40,000 after an onslaught of damaging articles. Ronnie regularly denied any sort of relationship or blackmail throughout his life, although he never commented on whether or not the orgies happened.

Reggie and Frances' flat in Cedra Court also received a lot of unwanted publicity after Frances took her own life. Of all of the puzzle pieces of their lives, the relationship between Frances and Reggie is perhaps the hardest to dissect.

Reggie was romantic when it came to Frances. This is something many people found hard to believe given the nature of his business. In the film *Legend* – in which their relationship is a central theme – many people were enamoured with them. At the end of this film, it depicts Reggie hitting and raping Frances at Cedra Court. Many of the closest family and friends to the couple said he never physically hurt her. Her family say he psychologically wore her down over the years, though. Many of his mind games were said to have taken place in Cedra Court.

Like Ronnie, Frances suffered from a range of mental health issues throughout her life, all centring around depression. Frances never wanted Reggie to live the life he did. She documented her time in Cedra Court extensively in a diary. Excerpts such as:

> He came in late every night drunk. Got up every morning two minutes to dress, left me all day and came back late at night drunk.

And,

> Him and a friend took me to the hospital, he was swearing and shouting at me in the car.

Many people believe that Frances was told to write her negative experiences with Reggie in a diary in order to aid their divorce proceedings as large portions of her daily entries were overwhelmingly negative.

The diary shows that she spent most of her time alone at Cedra Court. Although this flat may've held more positive memories for the twins, for Frances it was a sad place.

# Chapter 17

# 34 Wimborne Court

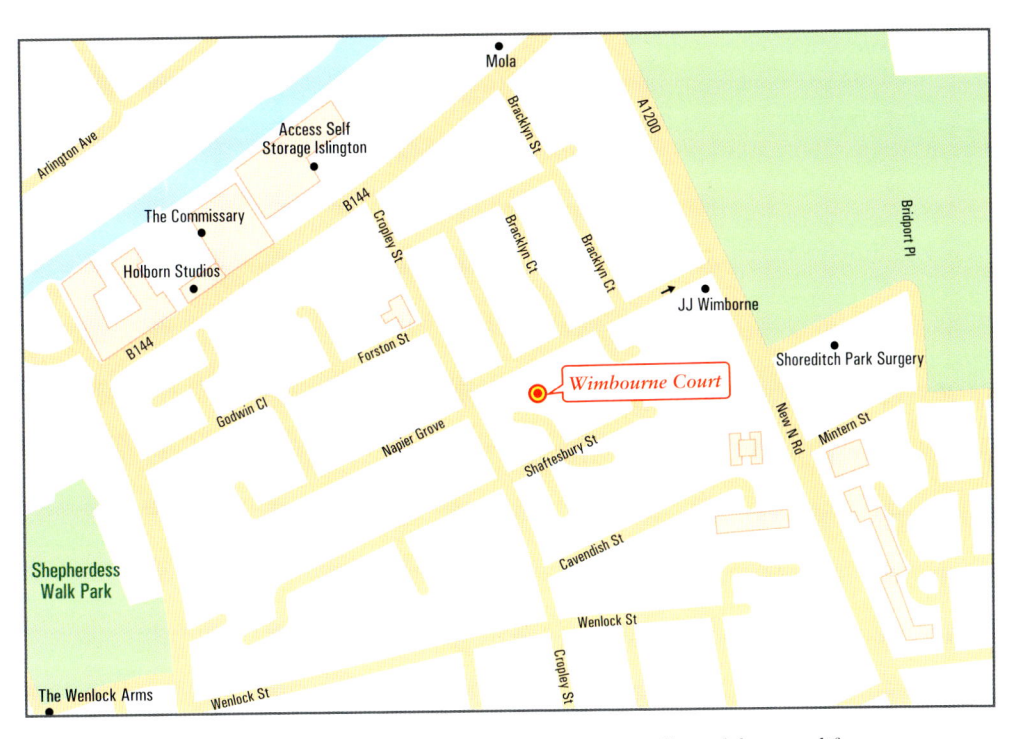

*34 Wimbourne Court, Frank Shea's flat, where Frances Kray tragically took her own life.*

**Where?**
34 Wimbourne Court
Wimbourne Street
Hoxton
Hackney
London
N1 7HB

**Why?**
This was the flat Frank Shea shared with his wife. It was also the location of Frances Shea's suicide in 1967.

**How to get there:**
Wimbourne Court has three stations within just under a mile from the block of flats. Angel Underground station and Hoxton station are good options, but Essex Road station is the closest with Wimbourne Court being a fifteen minute walk (0.8 miles). As you leave the station, walk across the road and straight onto New North Road. You'll remain on this road for most of your journey. After you've crossed the bridge, take the first right onto the B144 and the second left onto Cropley Street. Take the second left onto Wimbourne Street, and Wimbourne Court is visible from the end of the road.

34 Wimbourne Court was the flat Frank Shea moved into – with his new wife – after he moved out of his parents' house in Ormsby Street. This unassuming flat became an integral part of the lives of Frances and Reggie Kray after Frances moved out of her flat in Cedra Court and into Frank's flat because of the marital problems between her and Reggie.

When Frank moved into the six-storey block of flats with his wife, they were fairly new and they've barely changed in appearance since. At the time, tower-block style flats were a new concept; the first was built in Harlow, Essex, in 1951. In many cases, these buildings were seen as a quick fix to solve a multitude of housing problems that arose in post-war London. Firstly, with the population growing, being able to fit people into smaller flats and work upwards instead of outwards was seen as a great advantage. Secondly, many old buildings in London were crumbling wrecks and with the East End of London growing evermore popular, the government agreed that building more of the same terraced houses wouldn't work to future-proof the area. Many of the Krays' friends and family were moved out of their terraced, war-damaged houses to make way for these new blocks of flats. At the time, the flats were seen as an enticing prospect for people living in unsanitary conditions, particularly because they offered some of the best views and vantage points across the whole of London.

Although this was seen as a quick fix at the time, nowadays many of these areas have seen a rise in crime and are considered undesirable places to live. In turn, many of these flats have been turned into social housing.

This tower block is classic of the 'building boom' which took place post-war. The government was eager to show local people that they were making progress in repairing their livelihoods. As a result, the mandate from the government to the construction companies was to make the buildings look futuristic and incite a buzz among the otherwise worn-down local communities in the East End of London. This futuristic style of architecture was the Brutalist method which favoured stark slabs of exposed concrete and was seen by the younger generation of architects as a contrast to the frivolity of 1930s' housing. Unfortunately, this particular style of building didn't remain popular for too long and has been critiqued in the modern day as being uninviting.

The flats are quite big for their time period and typically have three bedrooms. When sold today, residents expect to get around £450,000 for one, due mainly to its prime Hoxton location. The grounds and the building itself remain very similar to how they would have looked in the 1960s and the walk up to number 34 is almost identical to the one Frank, his wife, and Frances would have taken.

At the time, Frank was pleased to be moving into this building. With only six floors, the views wouldn't be spectacular, but for most it was seen as quite the upgrade from their previous lifestyle; the flats, in this respect, served their purpose. It wasn't long after Frank had moved in that Frances followed.

This move wasn't the first of Frances' bids to escape. Two months after Frances and Reggie got married, she began psychiatric treatment at Hackney Hospital. In the eighteen months that followed their wedding, Frances tried to commit suicide twice.

In the inquest into her death – in which she was notably referred to as Frances Shea – Dr Julian Silverstone, a consultant psychiatrist at Hackney Hospital, said she was admitted to hospital in June 1966 and remained there until September the same year. After her release, she was admitted to St Leonard's Hospital in October 1966 after she overdosed on barbiturates – a sedative drug regularly prescribed for anxiety.

Then, in January 1967, she was admitted to St Leonard's Hospital once again after she was found unresponsive in a gas-filled room. On both occasions, she left a suicide note, although the details of the note remain unknown.

On 7 June 1967, on her third attempt, Frances killed herself at Wimbourne Court after taking another overdose of barbiturates. Her brother, Frank, found her. Reggie, who was told shortly afterwards by Frances' family, rushed over to see her.

Dr Julian Silverstone agreed with the Coroner that she had a 'personality disorder' which ultimately led to her numerous suicide attempts. The Shea family believed that Reggie played a large part in her emotional issues, although Frank Shea was largely quiet during these interviews and comments. Frank told the coroner that Frances was hoping for reconciliation with Reggie. Over the years, Frank didn't speak to the media about his feelings towards Frances' death; his family – namely his mother – was more vocal and Frances' extended family have rallied for a name change on her gravestone for many years.

# Chapter 18

# The Lion

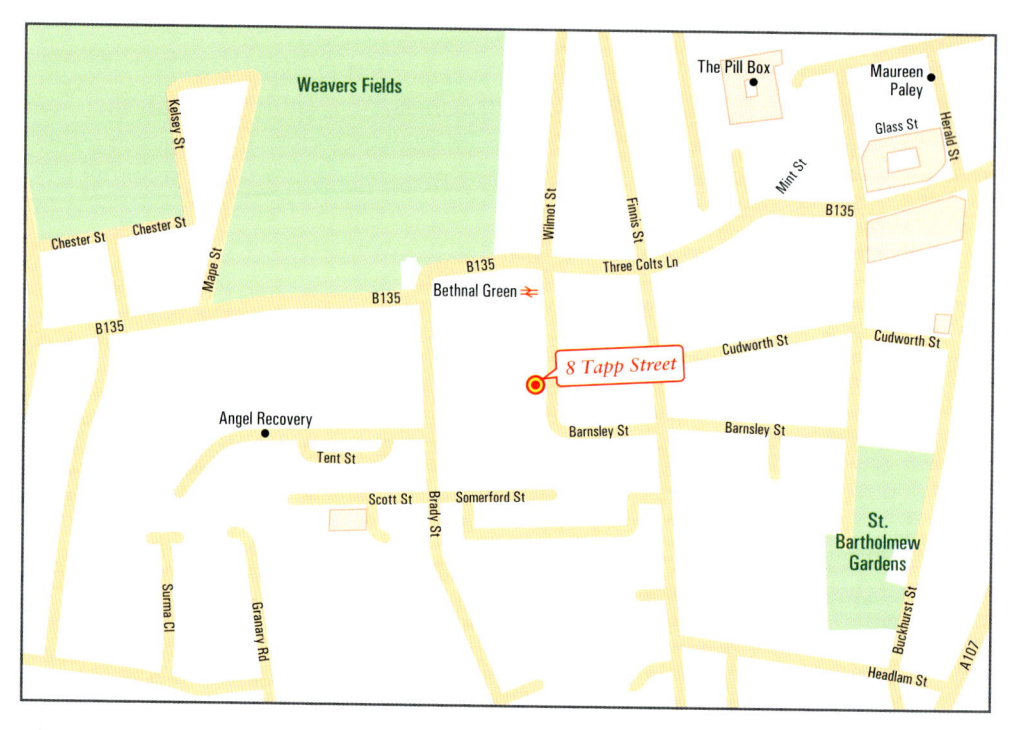

*The Lion; the pub where Ronnie was drinking before he headed to the Blind Beggar to confront George Cornell.*

**Where?**
8 Tapp Street
Bethnal Green
London
E1 5RE

**Why?**
It was rumoured that the Krays kept a whole room of weaponry and such in a back room of this pub. Their close association with the landlord was seen by locals as very suspicious.

## *The Lion*

**How to get there:**
This pub – which is now a residential building, is situated very close by to Bethnal Green Overground station. Dependent on which exit you use to leave the station, you may find yourself already on Tapp Street. If not, just take a left and walk round the corner. Follow this road for one minute and you will see the old building on the right.

Given its proximity to Vallance Road (it's a seven-minute walk), The Lion was regularly visited by the Kray twins. This backstreet pub was nestled in one of the poorest areas of Bethnal Green. During the building's time as The Lion, it wasn't seen as a nice establishment; locals knew it as a place to avoid and where criminal activity would frequently take place.

The locals also knew it as 'The Widow's Pub'. It had been taken over from the previous owner by his widow, she was called Marge and treated Ronnie and Reggie as if they were her own. Over the years, the Krays became more and more embedded in the place. Some locals said they believed the Krays actually owned the pub for a while.

The Krays liked to strike a friendship with landlords of pubs. There have been at least a dozen examples of this during their monopoly over East London. By building this friendship, people believed they would feel more comfortable asking the landlords to store things for them and asking to use the rooms for meetings. Although it is believed that Ronnie and Reggie stored various loots from their dealings in pubs and other establishments across London, this is something the pair have never discussed with the media.

When Ronnie and Reggie were spending a lot of time in The Lion, many locals believed there was a higher purpose than because they liked it as a place to have an afternoon pint. This theory grew in Bethnal Green largely because The Lion wasn't seen as an upmarket place to visit. Ronnie and Reggie never let go of their East End roots throughout their lives, so it wasn't a case of them becoming too rich or successful to frequent a pub like this. The theory was mostly born from the fact that even the hardy locals who came from the poorest roads in the area didn't particularly like drinking there.

Armed with this theory, the Richardson Gang were planning a raid on The Lion. It was rumoured that the Krays kept weapons in one of the back rooms, although this has never been confirmed by anybody close to the Krays. The Richardson Gang's feud with The Krays is widely documented and both sides suffered from many casualties and even fatalities because of the ongoing battle. The gang was headed by Charlie and Eddie Richardson, brothers from Brentford, West London.

Hearing of this rumoured raid, the Krays struck pre-emptively and raided Mr Smith's Club in Catford as a retaliation of sorts. In the process, one of the Krays' friends, Richard Hart, was killed.

The night after Hart's murder, Ronnie Kray was drinking heavily in The Lion before making a spur of the moment decision to murder George Cornell, another active member of The Richardson clan – who he knew was drinking at The Blind

Beggar, a mere six minute walk from The Lion. Ron's right-hand man, Ian Barrie, drove Ron from The Lion back to 178 Vallance Road to pick up his gun. It's then believed he drove back to The Lion after the murder to finish his pint.

The building is almost identical to how it looked in the 1960s. The bottom third of the building has now been painted blue; it was a dark green in previous years. Although there's no obvious signs that it used to be a pub on the frontage, if you walk round to the right of the building (as you look at it) to the wall facing the railway arch, you'll notice there's still a Truman's notice board on the wall.

# Chapter 19

# The Blind Beggar

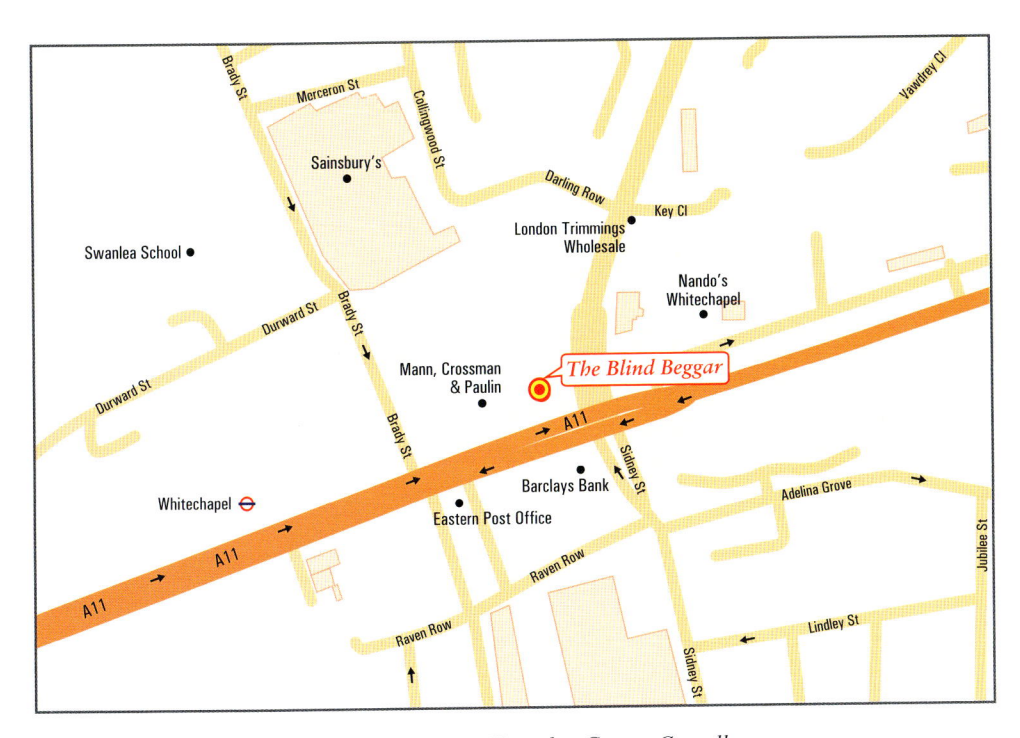

*The Blind Beggar, the famous pub where Ronnie Kray shot George Cornell.*

### Where?
337 Whitechapel Road
Stepney
London
E1 1BU

### Why?
The Blind Beggar pub is one of the most historic landmarks when looking into the lives of the Krays. It's where Ronnie Kray killed George Cornell in front of dozens of witnesses.

**How to get there:**
The Blind Beggar is a short walk from Whitechapel Underground station but can also be reached quite easily from Central London. In fact, you can see the skyline of the city as you stand outside of the pub. From Whitechapel Underground station, exit onto Whitechapel Road. Turn left and walk 0.1 miles (two minutes) and you will find The Blind Beggar on the left. It's situated on the corner.

The Blind Beggar pub is a must-visit for anybody interested in the criminal history of the Kray twins. The pub is perhaps the most obvious association to the pair, particularly Ronnie, and it's the place people tend to remember when talking about the Kray twins. It's certainly one of the most well-documented.

It was a regular haunt for both Ronnie and Reggie. They would meet up with other well-known gangsters who operated in their gang. Other criminals also visited The Blind Beggar, too. Due to its location and the unassuming nature of the pub, it made the perfect meeting point for criminal dealings.

Before the Krays frequented the pub, it was known as the location that William Booth, the founder of the Salvation Army, held his first sermon. This sermon consequently led to the creation of the Salvation Army.

The pub became a place of mass interest on 9 March 1966. When Ronnie Kray entered the pub, George Cornell, who was a member of The Firm's rivals, The Richardson Brothers, was already at the bar. George Cornell started to mock Ronnie; by now we know a lot about Ronnie's mental instability, so this type of public embarrassment wasn't going to end well. Ronnie shot George there and then and he died later that night in hospital.

There were conflicting views about why Ronnie decided to shoot George so publicly, given that the Krays were quite careful to watch their tracks before this point. At a Christmas party at the Astor Club in 1965, George Cornell had called Ronnie Kray a 'fat poof', which led to a fight. Some people believe Ronnie was still holding a grudge about this event. Others believe Ronnie Kray wanted to send a clear message to the Richardson Brothers about who was boss.

It wasn't until Ronnie Kray later wrote 'In front of a table full of villains, George Cornell called me a "fat poof". He virtually signed his own death warrant', in the Krays' book *Our Story*, that the shooting became clearer.

The Richardson/Kray feud was widely noted. The Richardson Brothers were known as the 'Torture Gang' whose alleged methods included using pliers to pull out teeth, using bolt cutters to cut off toes, and nails to nail people to the floor.

The feud began in Winchester Prison, when Charlie Richardson and George Cornell first met the Krays. The two gangs ended up engulfed in a turf war that lasted much of the 1960s.

The former jewel thief, Lenny Hamilton, who had quite a few run-ins with Ronnie Kray over the years, spoke openly about the feud in the years leading to his death in 2014. He suggested the beginning of the disagreements between Ronnie and George Cornell actually started when Cornell won a fistfight outside The Brown Bear pub in Leman Street, Whitechapel, knocking Ronnie unconscious. Supposedly, this was the one and only time Ronnie had lost a fistfight and it had left quite an emotional scar as a result.

On the days leading up to George Cornell's shooting, Richard Hart, who was an associate of the Krays, was shot dead during a brawl at Mr Smith's Club in Catford. The exact truth surrounding the shooting is unknown, with many of the gang members having differing accounts of what happened. It was evident, however, that the turf battle was coming to a head.

After Ronnie shot George Cornell, it is reported that he shot the ceiling several times to warn people off of reporting this incident to the police. Although there were four eye-witnesses in the pub at the time, nobody would testify against Ronnie. The two friends of George – Albie Woods and Johnny Dale – who were drinking with him, slipped out the back of the pub before they could be called up as witnesses. The barmaid said she didn't see who did it and an old man drinking there at the time famously said 'I hate the sight of blood, particularly my own', when asked to testify against Ronnie.

Everybody in the East End knew Ronnie had killed George. George's wife, Olive, turned up at 178 Vallance Road and ended up throwing a brick through the window in anger at what Ronnie had done.

The pub is best known for its association with the Kray twins, but it has a rather decorated history in its own right. As well as holding William Booth's first sermon, it was also the birthplace of the first brown ale at the beginning on the twentieth century.

Contrary to popular belief, the murder of George Cornell was not the first event of its kind that tarnished the reputation of the Stepney establishment. Around 1904, there were a group of pickpockets who operated around the Stepney area and branded

## The Blind Beggar

themselves 'The Blind Beggar Gang'. A member of the gang, Bulldog Wallace, stabbed another man in the eye with an umbrella. So began a number of years of notoriety which ended with the killing of George Cornell.

The heavily renovated pub is almost unrecognisable in comparison to how it looked when George Cornell was shot, but there are subtle nods to the pub's past dotted all over the walls. It's very popular with tours and individuals alike who want to immerse themselves in the lives of the gangsters. It's a place to have a drink and look around at all of the memorabilia. It also has London's largest beer garden, so it gets rather busy on a warm day.

The frontage of the pub remains exactly the same as it was on the night of George Cornell's murder, giving you a real sense of what it felt like when Ronnie barged out of the swinging doors and into the streets. Given how many witnesses were on Whitechapel Road, it was quite remarkable that his arrest took three years.

# Chapter 20

# 206a Barking Road

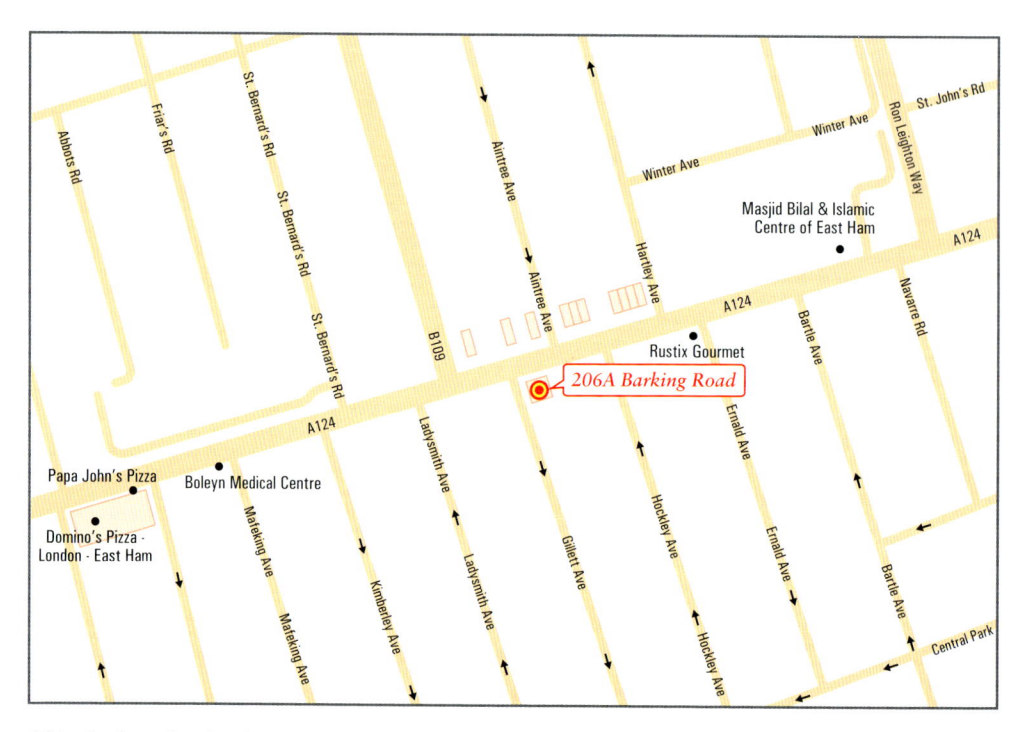

*206a Barking Road; where Ronnie and Reggie hid Frank Mitchell, also known as 'The Mad Axeman', after breaking him out of Broadmoor.*

**Where?**
206a Barking Road
East Ham
London
E6 3BB

**Why?**
206a Barking Road played a vital part in the final days of Frank Mitchell's life. Although it is not known whether he was killed or is still alive, he was last seen at this property in 1966.

## *206a Barking Road*

**How to get there:**
Barking Road is a thirteen-minute (0.6 mile) walk from East Ham Underground station. It's worth a visit because it has hardly changed since Frank Mitchell's last days living there. Walk out of the station and take a left on High Street North. Take a right at Ron Leighton Way and follow this road until you reach Barking Road. Take a right. 206a Barking Road is situated on the left-hand side of the road on the corner of Barking Road and Gillett Avenue.

Although many people interested in the history of the Kray twins may not have heard of 206a Barking Road, it's likely they've heard of Frank Mitchell – or, 'The Mad Axeman'. 206a Barking Road plays a key role in the story of the Kray twins' relationship with this notorious criminal.

To supplement this story, let's first learn a little about Frank Mitchell and how the Kray twins found themselves involved with him. His life – from the age of 9 – featured numerous run-ins with the law. In 1955, after several spates in prison, Frank Mitchell was diagnosed as 'mentally defective'. After this diagnosis, he spent time in Rampton Psychiatric Hospital but escaped after a short while. When the police attempted to recapture him, he attacked them with meat cleavers and was sent to Broadmoor.

Frank Mitchell made a habit of escaping prisons, and he managed to escape from Broadmoor shortly after his arrival. This time, he broke into a home and held a couple hostage with an axe, which is where his nickname 'The Mad Axeman' came from. After this misdemeanour he was sentenced to life imprisonment to be carried out at Broadmoor.

Ronnie Kray met Frank Mitchell when their sentences overlapped at Wandsworth Prison in the 1950s. They were close; close enough that Ron hired a lawyer for Frank during one of his trials. Reggie also knew Frank well and during his numerous visits to see Ronnie in prison, he too became quite close to The Mad Axeman.

It wasn't, however, until Frank asked Ronnie to break him out of Broadmoor for the second time that their friendship took a turn. This prison breakout was extremely well-publicised, but there are two vastly different versions of events on offer, even to this day.

What everybody involved in this break-out can agree on is that on 12 December 1966, three members of The Firm, Albert Donoghue, Teddy Smith and Billy Exley broke Frank Mitchell out of prison by order of the Kray twins.

By all accounts, the break-out was a fairly simple affair. Ronnie regularly remarked on the ease in which Frank Mitchell was able to wander off to nearby towns in the time he was in Broadmoor so when he asked one of the security guards if he could 'feed the ponies' they readily agreed. He walked out into the moors and straight into a waiting car containing The Firm's three most trusted members.

There's much debate to be had about why a highly dangerous criminal was able to escape, but it is said that many of the prisoners (particularly long-time offenders) were given special privileges if they behaved themselves. One such privilege involved feeding the ponies and tending to the fields in the areas of Broadmoor that weren't protected by security fencing.

Everybody involved also agreed that from there he was driven to a safe house belonging to Lennie Dunn, who was a friend of Charlie Kray. This flat was 206a Barking Road. Once inside, Teddy Smith – who was the best writer in The Firm – wrote a letter to the Home Secretary in a bid to have Frank's case looked at. They claimed that if the government would just look at his case, he would return voluntarily to Broadmoor. They also sent a copy of the letter to the *Daily Mirror* and *The Times*, both of whom published it. The Home Secretary didn't respond, which left Frank Mitchell and the Krays in no man's land; Frank Mitchell was unable to leave Lennie Dunn's flat and the Krays were becoming increasingly impatient with his erratic ways.

It's at this point that two very different stories emerge. One story belongs to the Kray twins, the other belongs to a select group of now ex-The Firm members. Ronnie Kray's version of events is simple: after they didn't hear back from the Home Secretary, Frank was taken – by boat – into Europe. He believed at the time of writing in his autobiography *Our Story* that Frank Mitchell was still alive and living somewhere – anywhere – in the world with a new identity.

The second version of events was one that was rigorously debated in court. Members of The Firm Albert Donoghue, Freddie Foreman and Alfie Gerrard told Frank Mitchell he was to join them in a van to be escorted to Ron Kray's Suffolk 'hide out' to keep him safe from the law as 206a Barking Road was becoming a place of interest to the police. As soon as he was in the van, Freddie Foreman and Alfie Gerrard shot at him with a revolver.

Just eleven days after he was freed, Ronnie, Reggie, Charlie, Pat Connolly and Freddie Foreman were arrested for his murder. Albert Donoghue, a trusted associate until this point, testified against them at the Old Bailey. Albert claimed he heard twelve shots fired before Frank Mitchell died. They were all found not guilty and Albert Donoghue's testimony was deemed as unreliable. Reggie Kray did, however, receive five years (that ran alongside his other sentences) for conspiring to effect Frank's escape.

In Freddie Foreman's 1996 autobiography, *Respect*, he admits to 'shooting Frank Mitchell as a favour to The Krays'. He even announced his murder on TV in 2000, saying that Mitchell's body was bound with chicken wire, weighed down and dumped in the English Channel. As a result of Freddie's admission, he was questioned again by the police but the case wasn't reopened due to the double jeopardy law which was still in place during the time of his questioning.

It's curious, as an outsider, why Ronnie and Reggie Kray who cited themselves as such great friends of Frank Mitchell would decide to kill him. Over the years, details of this have emerged. If Freddie Foreman's admissions are true, they decided to kill him because he was becoming a nuisance. Contrary to the opinions they voiced, Frank Mitchell was a dangerous criminal; he was hot-headed, short-tempered and physically very strong. When the pair said it was too risky for him to leave 206a Barking Road he became agitated and made threats against the Krays. It was this – according to ex-members of The Firm – that led to the twins believing that killing him was the only viable option.

## *206a Barking Road*

206a Barking Road is still intact and almost identical to how it looked in 1966. The unassuming flat was offered up by Lennie Dunn – a market stall owner who was desperate to become a part of the inner circle of The Firm. His wife left him shortly before this decision, so it was decorated with a woman's touch. It was a homely place filled with flowers, ornaments and floral wallpaper, quite the contrast to The Mad Axeman hiding inside it.

During Frank Mitchell's short stay, it was suggested by Ronnie and Reggie that he spent it with a woman. They picked out Lisa Prescott, a young nightclub hostess, and paid her for her troubles. She ended up spending four days solid in 206a Barking Road and it's said that Frank Mitchell started to fall for her, which only compounded the Krays' fear that he was becoming a nuisance.

# Chapter 21

# The Regency

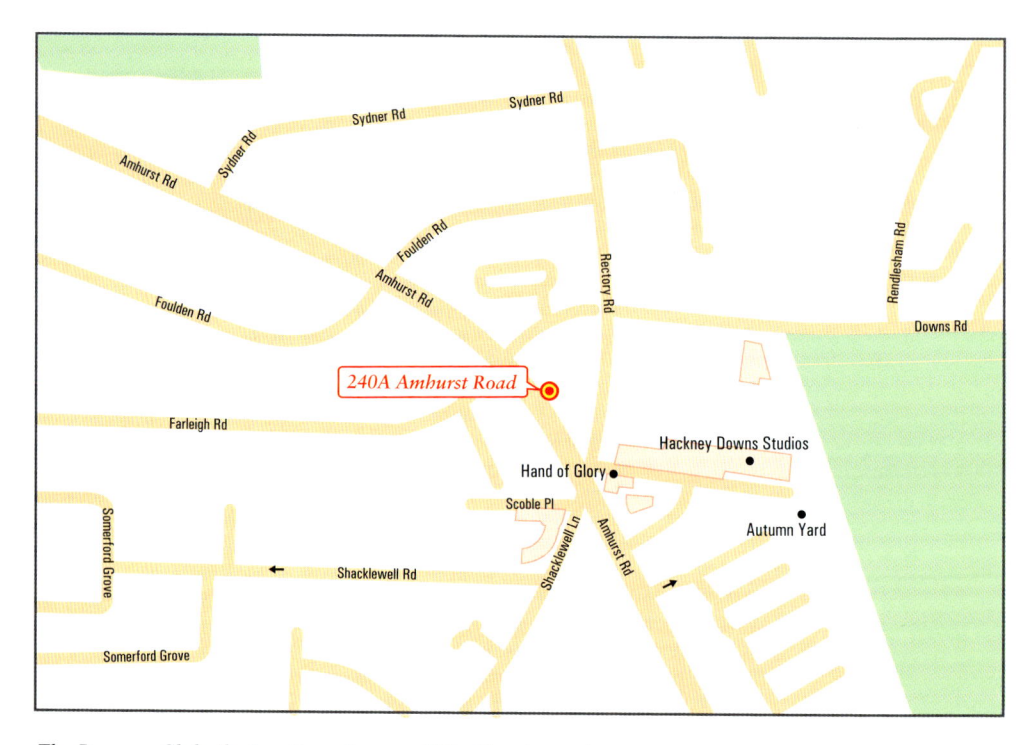

*The Regency Club, the location of many of The Firm's meetings.*

**Where?**
240a Amhurst Road
Stoke Newington
London
E8 2BN

**Why?**
Towards the end of the Krays' reign over East End London, The Regency was one of their favourite haunts. Its close proximity to Cedra Court was likely to have something to do with this.

## *The Regency*

**How to get there:**
This visit can be teamed with a visit to Evering Road and Cedra Court. The nearest station is Rectory Road. Take a right on Evering Road and then take the first left onto the A10. Follow this road and keep on it as it changes into Rectory Road. Follow this road all the way down to the crossroads where it turns into Shacklewell Lane and turn right onto Amhurst Road. 240a Amhurst Road can be found in between Rectory Road and Farleigh Road.

At the end of the 1960s, Stoke Newington started playing quite a key role in the lives of the Kray twins, this shift in focus is likely down to the close proximity to Cedra Court; it's just one mile away from their base in Cazenove Road. The first spot of interest in this part of London is The Regency, which was a small nightclub and restaurant popular during the Krays' reign.

It was owned by John and Anthony Barry. The pair were close friends of the twins and paid them protection money in order to ward off any other criminals. It's reported that the Barry brothers paid The Krays £50 per week to look after their club.

The club and restaurant was a relatively peaceful one throughout the early 1960s; it was a regular haunt of Princess Margaret and Lord Boothby. It had gained a name as being a neutral ground for the big names in the criminal underworld, which kept the day-to-day running of the place quite simple. That was, of course, until the feud between Jack McVitie, a man the Krays regularly employed to conduct criminal activity on their behalf, and Reggie Kray started to intensify (read more about this conflict and how The Regency played a key role in it by reading 97 Evering Road).

The Regency Club's relaxed atmosphere started to dissipate towards the end of the 1960s. Pat Connolly, who was a member of The Firm, Bonner Ward – son of Buller Ward who was a friend of the Krays – and Bonner's girlfriend were having a drink in The Regency one evening. Lenny Hamilton, who was a jewel thief and acquaintance of the twins, made a beeline for the group and asked Bonner's girlfriend if she'd like a drink. In interviews since, Lenny Hamilton said he meant no malice by the question, but Bonner Ward didn't view the conversation in quite the same way.

The same evening, a brawl broke out in the toilets of The Regency whereby Bonner Ward lurched towards Lenny Hamilton with a razor blade. This dispute didn't go unnoticed by Ronnie Kray who, in turn, lured Lenny Hamilton to Esmeralda's Barn after hours and burned him with a white-hot poker stick.

The Barry brothers eventually sold this property, but that wasn't the end of its criminal associations. For thirty years after the Barry brothers, its reputation was – arguably – more alarming than in the days of Lenny Hamilton and Bonner Ward.

During this time, the club catered for a large number of gang members. It wasn't unusual to hear of a stabbing, a shooting or a large-scale gang fight in Amhurst Road. It only takes a quick Google of 'Amhurst Road' to really delve into the past. The primary reason behind the high levels of violence was the drug dealings that went on along the road. Residents of the time reported that they felt extremely vulnerable. Finally, in 2008, the license was revoked and the club became the entryway to a number of high-end apartments.

The building still remains largely intact, the art-deco frontage, which is composed of two pillars either side of the door and triangular stonework on top, is still present from the days of the Krays. The only notable difference is that the stone has been painted over and no longer features a black border in the coving. If doors could talk, this one would have quite a lot to say…

# Chapter 22

# The Carpenter's Arms

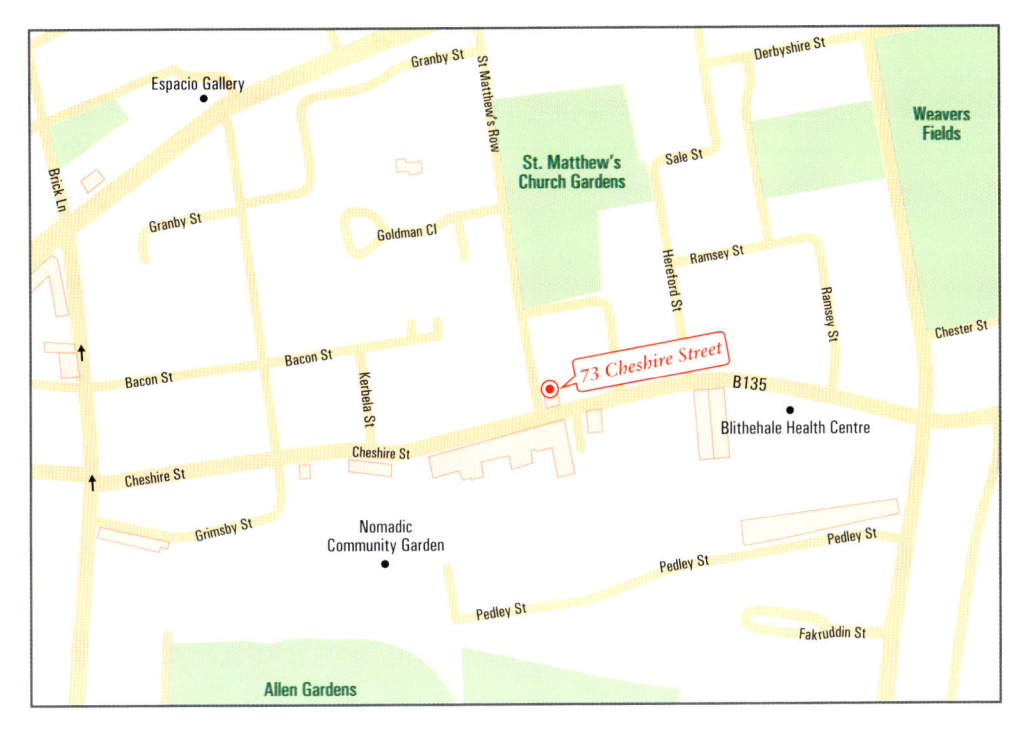

*The Carpenter's Arms, the pub the Kray twins bought for their Mother, Violet.*

**Where?**
73 Cheshire Street
Bethnal Green
London
E2 6EG

**Why?**
Due to its closeness to Vallance Road, The Carpenter's Arms was one of the Krays' favourite pubs.

**How to get there:**
Cheshire Street and the surrounding areas feature many of the most popular haunts of the Kray twins. Visit here when visiting Repton Boxing Club and St Matthew's Church. From Repton Boxing Club continue along Cheshire Street. You will also pass the frontage of William Davis Primary School on the left before reaching The Carpenter's Arms directly next to the school.

After The Blind Beggar, the Carpenter's Arms is perhaps the most well-known of the public houses the Kray twins frequented. It takes just a minute to walk there from Repton Boxing Club and 178 Vallance Road is also a stone's throw away. Their primary school – Wood Close School (now called William Davis Primary School) – is situated next door.

Cheshire Street is one of the most captivating roads to walk down in order to get a feel for the journey the Krays would've taken everyday. The pub became famous in 1967 when Ronnie and Reggie bought it for their mother, Violet. Given that the late 1960s were tumultuous years for them, they regularly enthused about the good times spent in this pub, which included many Christmas days and New Year's Eves.

As well as being a place of fun, The Carpenter's Arms was known as a place of business. Regularly, the doors would be closed to facilitate business meetings between Ronnie, Reggie and The Firm. The members of The Firm changed regularly, but there were a few recurring names. In the twin's book *Our Story* they're both open about the fact that in the end, the majority of The Firm let them down. Aside from Ronnie, Reggie and Charlie, some key members of the 'inner Firm' included: Reggie's right-hand man, Albert Donoghue, Ronnie's right-hand man, Ian Barrie, Pat Connolly, their bodyguard and Leslie Payne, their accountant who eventually gave evidence against the pair in their trial in 1969.

The way the pub was decorated by the Krays is one of the reasons it has been so popular with tourists over the years. Allegedly, the bespoke bar surface was made up of coffin lids. This has never been proven – nor disproven – but the bar surface from the time they were in residence is still intact today and is somewhat of a talking piece among visitors to the pub.

Aside from this slightly morbid urban myth, the rest of the decor was coherent with that of its time. It featured striped wallpaper and the pillars were painted burgundy, one of the most popular colours of the time. Even now, the new owners point to an area on one of the since-painted pillars which shows a chip through to the Burgundy decor of years gone by.

The Carpenter's Arms was, by all accounts, the Kray twins' home away from home. It was full of their own possessions, including their boxing gloves, which hung over the crest situated behind the bar. It was clear that Cheshire Road meant a lot to the family, when Reggie died, his procession went along the street for his funeral in October 2000.

In 2006, the pub was on the brink of being sold to be knocked down and redeveloped for residential usage. It was bought by the current proprietors who turned it into a gastropub, offering a host of ales to its trendy Shoreditch based clients. There's still a very clear Krays influence, though. There's a large abstract portrait of the pair on the wall as you enter the pub and in the room to the back, there's a glass cabinet filled with interesting memorabilia.

It's poignant to note that on the evening of 28 October 1967, Reggie went into The Carpenter's Arms for a drink before allegedly taking a carving knife from the kitchen and heading to 97 Evering Road…

# Chapter 23

# 97 Evering Road

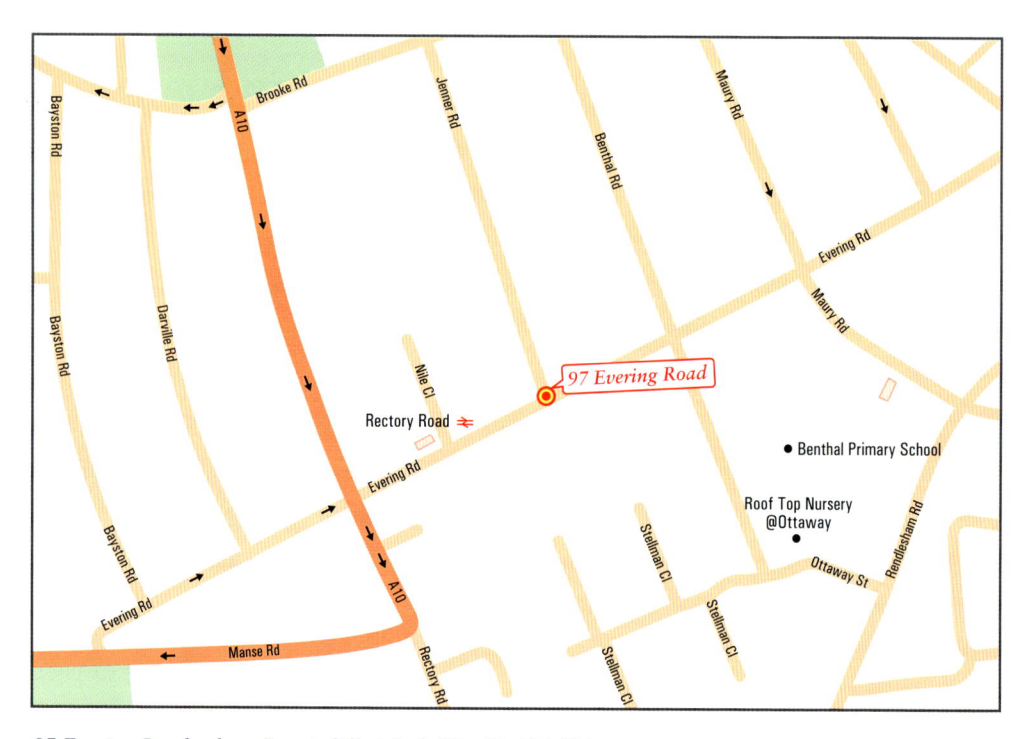

*97 Evering Road, where Reggie killed Jack 'The Hat' McVitie.*

**Where?**
97 Evering Road
Stoke Newington
London
N16 7SL

**Why?**
Jack McVitie was killed by Reggie Kray in this flat belonging to his friend, Carol Skinner.

## *97 Evering Road*

**How to get there:**
97 Evering Road is a short walk from Rectory Road station (the same station you will use when visiting The Regency). Instead of taking a right to head towards The Regency, go left on Evering Road. 97 Evering Road can be found on the corner of Jenner Road.

After the twins moved to Cedra Court, they both spent more time around Stoke Newington. There are a couple of places of interest in Stoke Newington. As well as 97 Evering Road, The Regency (240a Amhurst Road, Stoke Newington, London, E8 2BN), a small nightclub owned by the Barry brothers, was regularly visited by the pair. The Regency is now a selection of high-end residential flats, but the building is still intact.

Stoke Newington – and particularly 97 Evering Road – is key to the story of the Krays' London because of its association with Jack 'The Hat' McVitie.

Jack McVitie was hired by Ronnie and Reggie from time to time to do all manner of illegal dealings. From threatening business owners who hadn't paid their protection money to driving vans filled with contraband from one location to another. He was never a full-fledged member of The Firm, but he was regularly involved.

In 1967, he made a number of mistakes in the eyes of the Kray twins. Reggie cites two particularly occasions in which he had become a hindrance to the progress of The Krays' gang. The first was at a club in Stoke Newington; the owner had racked up around £1,000 in protection debt and Reggie and Jack went there to sort the issue out. The club owner had fallen upon hard times and offered Reggie £200 upfront with the rest to follow. According to Reggie's account, this satisfied him. But, without his permission, Jack pulled a gun and shot the man in the foot.

The second misdemeanour occurred when Jack was asked to pick up a van load of goods from a warehouse in Kent. Not trusting him, Reggie asked Ron's right-hand man, John Dickson, to trail him. It turned out that Jack McVitie was working with the warehouse foreman in Kent to double-cross the twins and sell the contraband goods elsewhere.

Jack McVitie's penchant for alcohol and drugs made him a liability. Some weeks after his warehouse dealings, he was telling anybody at The Regency who would listen how he'd managed to double-cross the Kray twins and how they were losing their touch. At one point during his rampage through The Regency, it's reported that he brandished a sawn-off shotgun at the owners of the club, demanding to know where the twins were because he wanted to kill them. During his drunken frenzies he would regularly threaten to kill the Kray twins, but never while they were in earshot.

Nipper Read, the policeman who was eventually responsible for the demise of the Kray twins, believed one of the primary reasons the Krays went to war on Jack McVitie was to do with Leslie Payne. According to Nipper Read, Ronnie and Reggie had ordered Jack to kill Leslie Payne, offering him £500 upfront with another £500 to come when the job was done. He never killed Leslie Payne, but kept the money.

It was these events that led up to 28 October 1967 and to 97 Evering Road. The basement flat of this impressive Victorian end-terrace house belonged to a friend of the twins, Carol Skinner; Carol was the cloakroom attendant at El Morocco and had regular parties in the flat. So, when Jack McVitie was lured there by some associates of the Kray twins who guised it as another of Carol's parties, he saw nothing of it.

The Kray twins asked Carol and her friends to go elsewhere while this exchange took place. As soon as Jack arrived, Reggie took a gun out and tried to shoot him twice in the head. The gun, however, jammed and McVitie tried to make a break for it. He tried desperately to dive out of the window, spraying glass everywhere, but he couldn't get out.

After pulling him from the window, one of the associates of The Firm handed Reggie a knife and held back McVitie's arms. Reggie stabbed him repeatedly in the face until he was dead.

From there, Ronnie and Reggie went to a friend's house in Hackney by car. After that, they personally disposed of the gun and the knife – which was later recovered – in the canal on Queensbridge Road, approximately 2 miles from Evering Road.

The house itself is still completely intact. It sits on the corner of Evering Road and Jenner Road; the basement window is even visible from street level, which gives a real sense of nostalgia around this awful event.

It was built in 1877 by William Osment, and Carol Skinner lived there for much of the 1960s. After the death of Jack McVitie, Carol continued to live in the flat, but all of the furniture, carpets and wallpaper were replaced, with members of The Firm sent in to redecorate.

# Chapter 24

# Grave Maurice

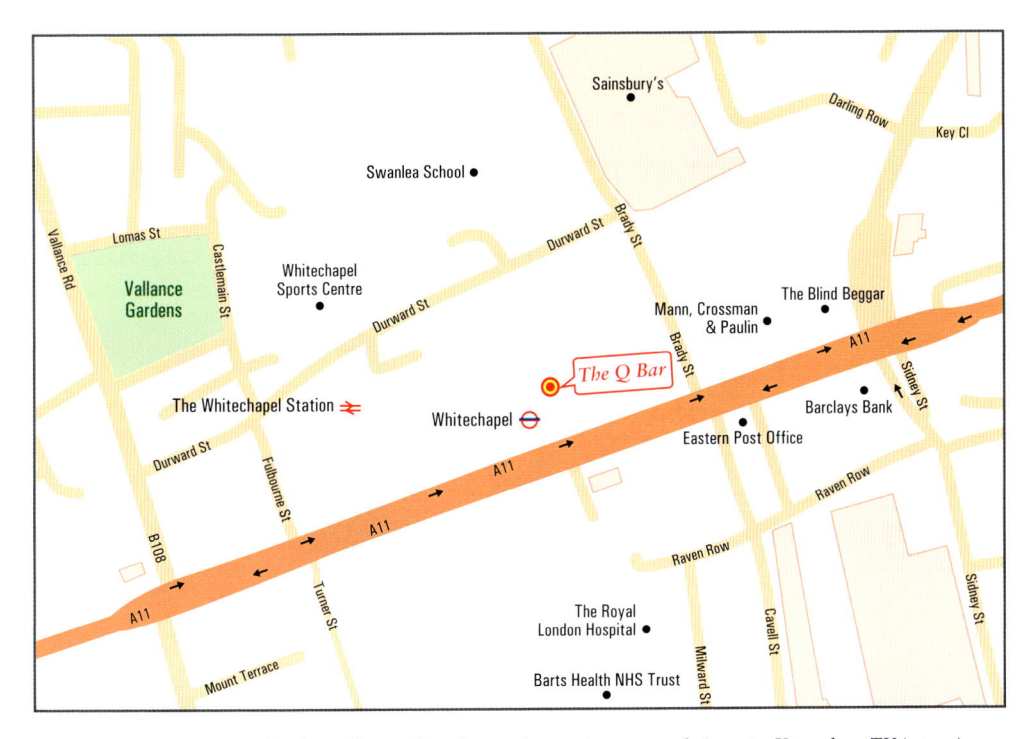

*Grave Maurice was a pub where Nipper Read went incognito to watch Ronnie Kray do a TV interview.*

**Where?**
Grave Maurice
269 Whitechapel Road
London
E1 1BY

**Why?**
The Grave Maurice was Ronnie's favourite pub. He often took media interviews in here and it's famously the place where the policeman who arrested him, Nipper Read, saw Ronnie for the first time.

**How to get there:**
The Grave Maurice is now a Paddy Power and is situated in between Whitechapel Underground station and The Blind Beggar. Leave Whitechapel Underground station and take a left, 269 Whitechapel Road is two doors down from the station.

People speculate about why Ronnie went to the Grave Maurice quite so often, saying that he liked it because you could sit at the bar and have a clear view of the door and – more importantly – who was walking through it. This, paired with the fact it was central to many of the Krays' operations, certainly played a part.

Just a short walk from Vallance Road, the pub was a popular haunt of the East End underworld. Aside from Ronnie's regular visits, gangsters like Frankie Fraser and George Cornell were patrons here in the early 1960s.

The history of this building starts way before the days of these London gangsters, though. It was originally built in 1723, but was rebuilt in 1874 in anticipation of an increased footfall as a result of the East London railway.

Like many of the pubs in the East End of London, it wasn't just gangsters of the Krays' era who spent time in this particular pub. It's interesting to note that pubs throughout the ages seem to get a reputation among criminals. All of Ronnie and Reggie's favourite pubs have had a history of criminal customers, the Grave Maurice is no exception.

Looking through the Old Bailey archives, it's evident there were some miscreants visiting the pub a long time before Ronnie and Reggie – and even their parents – were born.

In 1884, Timothy Tobin and John McNally were found guilty of grievously assaulting a customer after an evening in the Grave Maurice. Another local landmark referred to in the case – although there are no specifics as to why – was The Blind Beggar.

The pub became a little more than Ronnie's preferred place to drink in the late 1960s, when Nipper Read was on the case to bring down the twins. He'd learned that Ronnie was going to be doing a TV interview in the pub, so he arrived incognito to get a glimpse of his attitude and general demeanour. Catching him in his natural setting and behaving as he would on any other day was probably a great help to Nipper Read; it would have helped to build a profile of who Ronnie was and what made him tick.

A smart American car pulled up outside the Grave Maurice. As Nipper Read took his place in the window, he noticed that a well-dressed man got out of the car, visibly felt for his gun in his pocket, entered the Grave Maurice, looked around, went back outside and looked up and down the pavement and then finally, with a sweeping motion, opened the back door of the car.

Ronnie Kray stepped out of the car with a flourish, dressed like Al Capone. He made a grand entrance as a member of his entourage frisked the interviewer. After the interview had finished, Ronnie's 'team' went outside before him, checking the street before allowing him to enter onto it. This, many people have said, was quite a common occurrence as they walked into pubs and clubs. One interviewee said Ronnie and Reggie had an 'aura' which couldn't be ignored.

Despite its large size and seemingly ideal location, the pub itself has been described by numerous sources as a 'dive'.

The owners had the large downstairs area – which included a small, private lounge bar – as well as the upstairs areas. Upstairs it had a large snooker room, but aside from that, the upper levels hadn't been touched for a number of years. They were worn and in need of refurbishment.

The pub was decorated in quite a garish manner for an establishment of its time period. There were brass light-fixtures extending from ceilings and walls, and the most used materials were certainly leather and faux red velvet.

The pub hasn't just acted as a pilgrimage for people interested in the Kray twins over the years. In 1995, it became a hot spot for Morrisey fans after he was seen standing outside on the front cover of his album *Under The Influence*. Many people who visited it during that time period, though, said they were made to feel unwelcome, and so it struggled to make money off the back of these infamous associations.

In the late 2000s, it went through a short spell of being called Q Bar before being re-named back to Grave Maurice. As trade decreased, it finally closed in 2010 and was converted into a Paddy Power bookmakers. The upper floors are now flats, but the building, with its iconic arched windows, still looks very reminiscent of the time it spent as Grave Maurice.

There are a couple of nods to years gone by dotted around the building. Between the first and second floor, you might notice the signage 'Rebuilt The Grave Maurice An. Dm. 1874' which acts as a little reminder of its previous life.

# Chapter 25

# The Old Horns

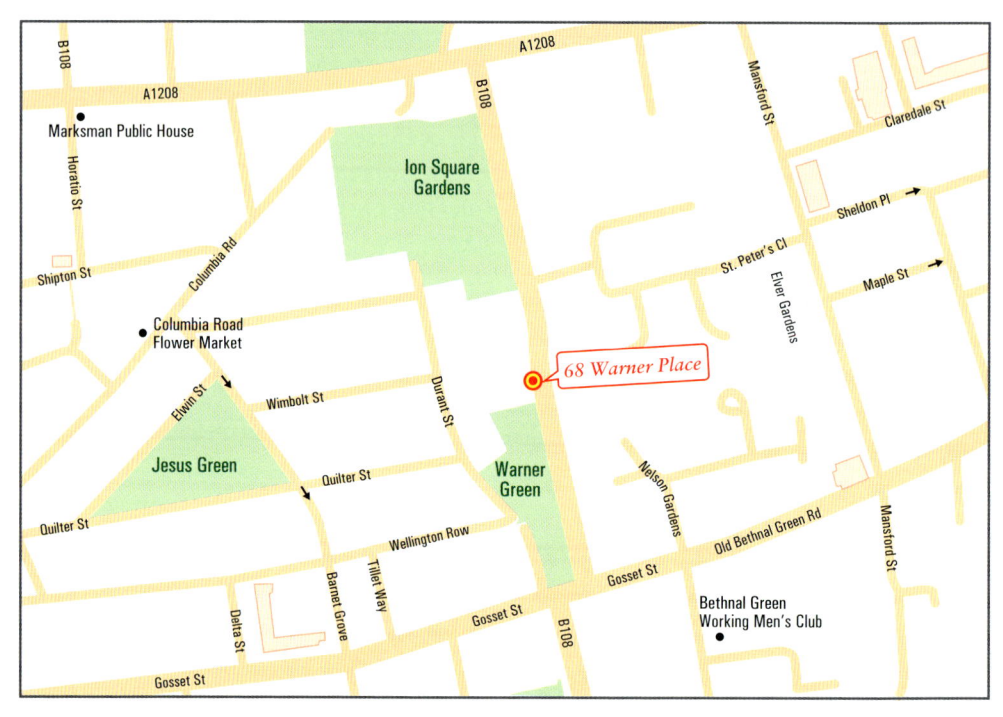

*The Old Horns, which is now a school, was where Ronnie and Reggie spent their last night of freedom.*

**Where?**
The Old Horns
68 Warner Place
Bethnal Green
London
E2 7DA

**Why?**
The Kray twins enjoyed a drink or two in this pub. It was owned by an old boxing friend of theirs, Teddy Berry.

*The Old Horns*

**How to get there:**
Warner Place is just off of Gosset Street and can be found most easily after a trip to nearby E. Pellucci. From E. Pellucci, take a left and then second right onto Squirries Street. Walk the length of Squirries Street and when you reach Gossett Street take a right. Take the first left onto Warner Place and 68 Warner Place is situated just under half way down the road.

The Kray twins worked out of, and spent time in, a number of pubs around the East End, but The Old Horns was a little further afield from their other regular haunts. The reason they ventured to this particular pub off Hackney Road is because it was owned by Teddy Berry, an old boxing friend of theirs.

Although Ronnie and Reggie had their favourites, it was evident that both them and The Firm would operate out of a large number of pubs in the Bethnal Green area. The reasoning behind this has never been confirmed, but a number of regular patrons of said pubs believed it was because they wanted to stay illusive. They were rarely all in the same place at the same time and from night to night they didn't tend to stick to the same establishment.

The Kray twins chose this pub to spend their last night of freedom in before returning to Violet and Charles' new flat in Braithwaite House. They didn't know this would be their last night of freedom, but at this point they had quite a good idea that the police were closing in on them.

Aside from this happier memory, The Old Horns was also the location for a rather violent evening involving Billy and Ron Webb. In the '90s Billy Webb was particularly vocal about his hatred of Ronnie and Reggie. Shortly after Ron died, Billy was quoted saying:

> Death was kind to Ronnie Kray. He deserved a lot more than he got. He got off lightly. It is said that Ronnie screamed out for his mother just before he died, but compared with what he inflicted on others he suffered no pain.

And,

> It is a pity they abolished the death penalty. This would have been right and just punishment in the case of the Krays and would have saved a lot of heartache and misery to many people who sat and watched the glamorisation of the twins in recent years.

Billy and Ron Webb operated in London at the same time as the Krays and their business model was remarkably similar. They both ran gambling clubs and protection rackets and led by fear. Billy Webb was an enforcer for the slum landlord, Peter Rachman. During my interviews, many of the East End people regarded Billy Webb – particularly – as a 'low-life criminal'.

The two sets of brothers came to blows in The Old Horns. The story is according to Billy's account in his book *Running With The Krays* – which is reference to the time he spent on the run from the army with them. Many critics have called the title of his book a 'sales ploy' because his involvement with the pair is minimal and due to the bad blood between them, the Krays are hardly mentioned in his book.

They were set upon by the twins in the Old Horns and outnumbered twenty to one; both the Webb brothers were badly beaten up. Billy believes that his brother Ron's early death is as a direct result of the fight that took place in The Old Horns.

The Krays also first met Tony Lambrianou in this pub. This was the first meeting to discuss his potential role in The Firm. Tony went on to work long-term for the Krays and served ten years in jail for his part in the murder of Jack McVitie. This was also a regular meeting place for the Kray twins and David Bailey – who ended up playing a key part in Frances and Reggie's wedding.

The violent history of The Old Horns is now a distant memory, though. Today, the building is home to Bethnal Green Montessori School. Before it turned into a school, it first changed its name to Warners, and then changed it again to Jeremiah Bullfrog.

Then in 1997 it was closed, like many other pubs in the area, due to the decrease in customers. As far as the building goes, the bricks and mortar are still there; the windows and doors are in the same place. Aside from that, though, the building underwent a transformation after its closure. The upper level was originally red brick and it's now grey cladding. The bottom of the building looked like a classic pub; painted white walls filled the upper section and the lower part was covered in black tiles. Now, this area has been plastered over to reveal a smooth grey finish.

# Chapter 26

# Braithwaite House

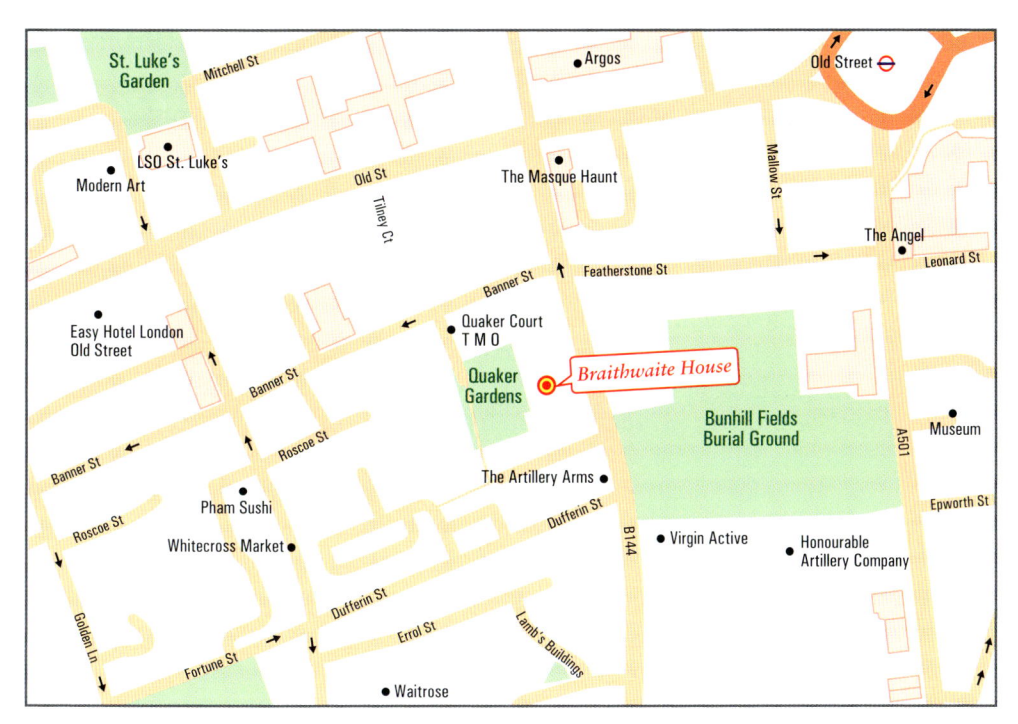

*Violet and Charles Kray were moved to Braithwaite House when 178 Vallance Road was demolished by the council in 1967.*

**Where?**
43 Braithwaite House
Bunhill Road
Shoreditch
London
EC1Y 8NE

**Why?**
After Violet and Charles Kray were moved out of Vallance Road, they were moved into Braithwaite House. Reggie and Ronnie became familiar with this block of flats, although it never replaced Vallance Road.

**How to get there:**
Braithwaite House is one of the most central spots. The nearest station is Old Street Underground station. From this station, take the exit onto Old Street and follow the road down until you reach Bunhill Row on the left. Braithwaite House is situated just after Banner Street on the right-hand side of the road.

In terms of architecture, Braithwaite House is a stark contrast to Vallance Road and yet, in 1967, Violet Kray moved to flat 43 on the ninth floor.

The nineteen-storey tower block looks as though it has been untouched between 1967 and the present day and visiting there offers up a real sense of 1960s architecture. This building, as were many others in the East End of London, was built as part of the urban development after the Second World War.

The architecture has moved on, and nowadays the breeze block, concrete and lack of balconies aren't in keeping with the modern style, but former residents of the building said it was a real treat to move there in the 1960s. Many of their council homes were run down following the effects of the war. The majority of the council houses – including Vallance Road – only had an outside toilet, so for each flat to have its own was considered a luxury.

When news of the demolition of Vallance Road spread to Violet and it was time for her and Charles to move to Braithwaite House, Violet became extremely emotional. Although the amenities in Braithwaite House were much improved, many people struggled to move away from houses they'd had for their entire lives. A large number of the East End population felt wronged by the council, after all, their family houses – which held so many memories – had survived the war. There was a sense of pride in the community after much of the East End was destroyed in the Blitz.

Nevertheless, Charles and Violet moved to Braithwaite House and the rest of the older members of the Kray clan were also forced to move as their areas faced demolition. The twin's grandparents – who were in their mid-eighties at the time, were moved to a maisonette on Cheshire Street and their beloved Aunt May was moved to Charles Dickens House in Mansford Street.

Although Braithwaite House never replaced Vallance Road, it did have some redeeming qualities. It overlooked the picturesque Bunhill Fields and the famous burial ground where the likes of William Blake and Daniel Defoe are buried.

Braithwaite House did, however, have to replace Vallance Road as the new headquarters of The Firm. The spacious living room easily accommodated the growing members of the operation.

It was also where the police picked both Ronnie and Reggie up in dawn raids after the murders of George Cornell and Jack McVitie. In their book, Ron says both he and his brother were picked up at Cedra Court, but during their trial, the police note that they were picked up at Braithwaite House after the twins had something of a party in a local pub the night before.

After Frances' death, both Ronnie and Reggie spent a lot more time at Vallance Road and then at Braithwaite House, so it's not unusual that the police located them there.

*Braithwaite House*

In more recent times, the tenants of Braithwaite House were involved in numerous debates about the building following the fire at Grenfell Tower which killed seventy-one people. As a result, the cladding that encased the building was removed. Many of the flats built as part of the regeneration of the East End plan after the war were built without the correct fire safety precautions, this included Braithwaite House.

# Chapter 27

# HM Brixton Prison

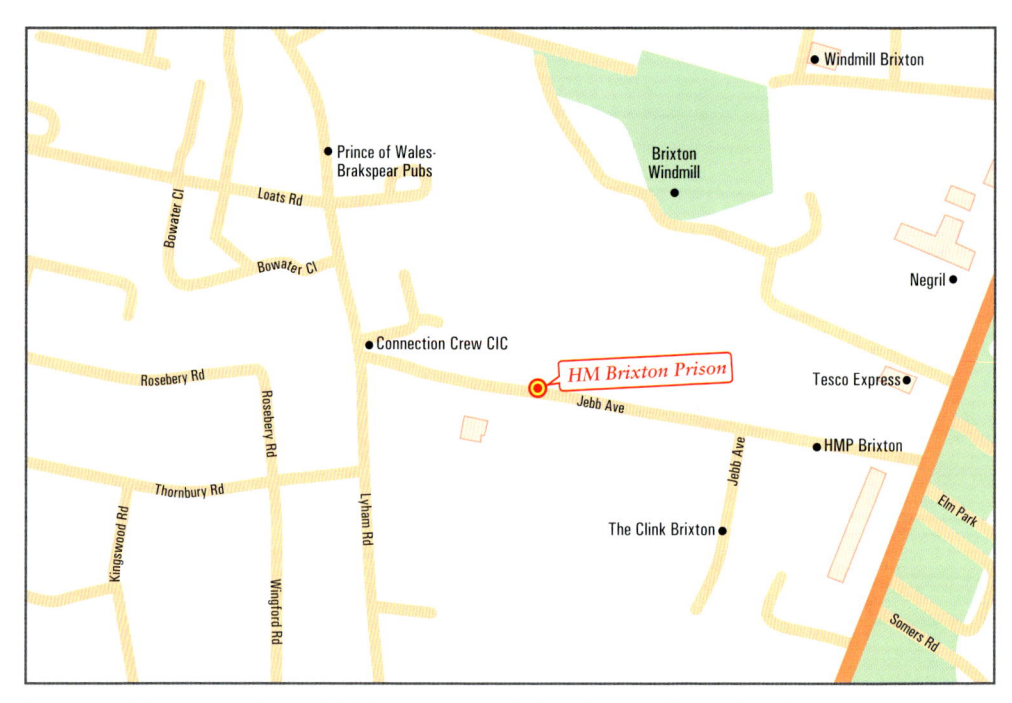

*Ronnie and Reggie were kept in HM Brixton Prison before their murder trial in 1968.*

**Where?**
Jebb Avenue
London
SW2 5XF

**Why?**
After Reggie and Ronnie were arrested for murder, they were held at HM Brixton Prison while they awaited trial.

**How to get there:**
HM Brixton Prison is a twenty-minute walk (0.9 miles) from Brixton station. Leave the station and take a left onto Brixton Hill. Follow this road all the way down until

you reach Jebb Avenue on your right. Follow this road and you will see HM Brixton Prison in front of you.

In May 1968, Ronnie and Reggie were arrested by Nipper Read – the key policeman on the murder investigation case. Ronnie had been arrested for the murder of George Cornell and Reggie for the murder of Jack McVitie. There were more than 100 police officers involved in the dawn raids on The Firm. At that point, it was the largest operation of its kind carried out by Scotland Yard.

There would be a preliminary hearing at Old Street magistrates' court, but before then, the pair were to be held in HM Brixton Prison. At the time of their arrival, Brixton Prison had just undergone a refurbishment. A new wing had been created with electric doors, which was seen as the future of prison life at the time. The pair were kept in adjoining cells, but their ability to communicate with each other was limited.

The original buildings of HM Brixton Prison date back to 1819. During the past two centuries, it has been everything from a military prison to a female-only prison. The Kray twins aren't the only notable inmates of years gone by. Mick Jagger as well as a variety of other public figures have served time in this establishment, too. It used to be a trial and remand prison up until 2012, and now it's classed as a resettlement prison. The frontage hasn't changed since the Krays were remanded here in 1968.

The pair managed to bribe two prison officers to give them information from both the outside world and about other inmates who were in HM Brixton Prison at the time. It was during that time that they struck up a friendship with Mad Frankie Fraser, who was a key part of the Richardson Gang. The friendship blossomed when Frankie offered to give evidence against George Cornell in Ron's case. At the time, Frankie was in prison because of the part he played in the war between the Krays and the Richardsons at Mr Smith's Club in Catford.

One by one, each member of The Firm was arrested. Just three of all the various associates employed by the Krays stayed loyal to them when they were pushed to give evidence and lighten their own sentences: Ian Barrie, Charlie Kray and Freddie Foreman.

During that time, the Krays had a smooth ride in HM Brixton Prison. Each day Violet Kray would travel from Braithwaite House to the prison – a 12-mile round trip – to bring in their lunch: cold chicken and salad and a bottle of wine.

By all accounts, including their own, the twins thought they were going to get away with murder – quite literally. They had many friends in to visit them: boxers, celebrities and public figures, and they didn't believe, despite the rumours, that members of The Firm were currently building a case against them. The public had such faith that they'd be found not guilty that local businesses were still paying protection money.

After their preliminary hearing at Old Street Magistrates' Court, the pair went back to HM Brixton Prison and stayed there until January 1969. In total, Ronnie and Reggie spent eight months in that particular prison awaiting trial.

# Chapter 28

# Old Street Magistrates' Court

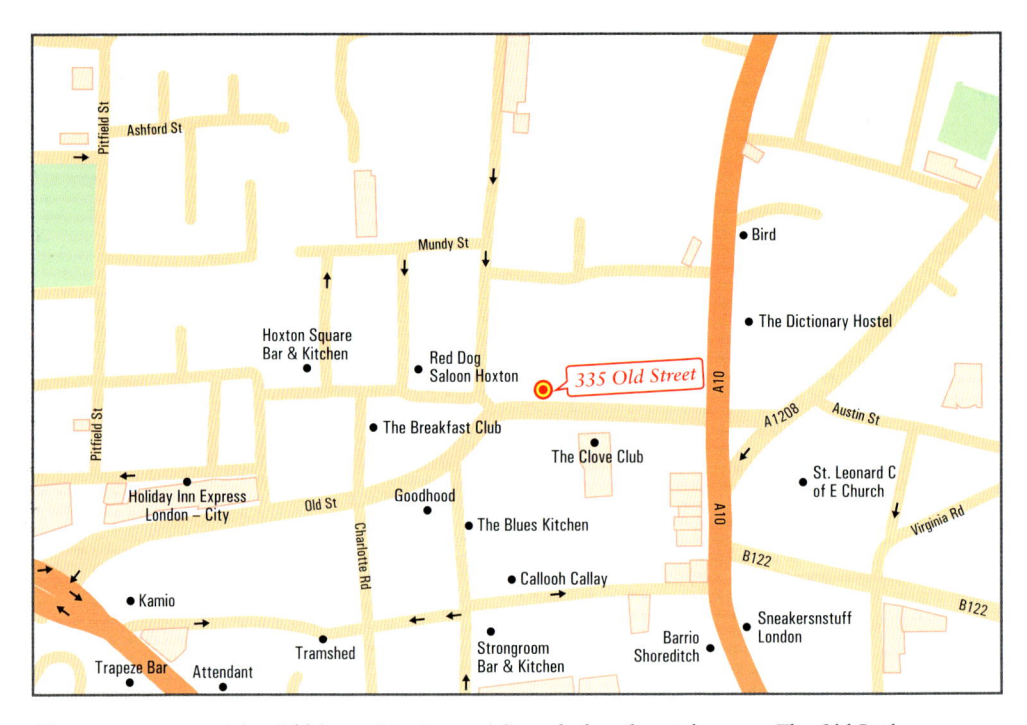

*The twins went on trial at Old Street Magistrates' Court before the trial went to The Old Bailey.*

**Where?**
335-337 Old Street
London
EC1V 9LL

**Why?**
The Kray twins went in front of a jury at Old Street Magistrates' Court twice during their lifetimes.

**How to get there:**
Pair in a trip to Braithwaite House with a trip to see Old Street Magistrates' Court. There is also a number of fantastic eateries around there, so be sure to factor in a food

stop. At Old Street station take the exit heading towards Shoreditch. Follow Old Street and be sure to stay on Old Street rather than following the natural curve in the road when it turns into Great Eastern Street. You will pass a range of restaurants on both sides of the road before reaching Old Street Magistrates' Court on the left.

Old Street Magistrates' Court played a key role in the demise of the Kray twins in the late 1960s. It was the location for their preliminary hearing and it took place on 6 July 1968, but they were also held there in 1965 for demanding money with menaces from Hew McCowan at The Hideaway (El Morocco).

There's film footage of the level of security around this hearing available, and it's quite staggering, even for today's standards. Scotland Yard had put a lot of time and money into this case and it was essential to the team leading the investigation that they achieved the result they were looking for. With Ronnie and Reggie's love for fooling officers and breaking themselves and other people out of prison, Scotland Yard took no chances.

The convoy that pulled up on Old Street consisted of at least a dozen motorcycles, numerous police cars and the van in which they were travelling. The security, police and public presence in Old Street was unlike any other case of its time.

The preliminary hearing at Old Street Magistrates' Court did not go well. Nipper Read called two witnesses: Billy Exley – who played a key role in breaking Frank Mitchell out of prison – and the barmaid who was working at the Blind Beggar on the night Ronnie shot George Cornell.

Afterwards, the twins were taken back to HM Brixton Prison and had to wait until January 1969 for their case to be referred to the Old Bailey.

The building was home to a court and police station from 1903–1996. The Kray twins aren't the only infamous inmates to walk through the doors; author of 1984 and Animal Farm, George Orwell (real name: Eric Arthur Blair), was also held here in 1931. Interestingly, he was picked up for being 'drunk and incapable', it transpired that George Orwell wanted to experience what being in a prison environment was like for a novel and so purposefully provoked the police into arresting him.

While the court left the building in 1996, the police station was not located elsewhere until 2008. After that time, this iconic building was used as a set for a number of films and TV programmes, notably Spooks and Luther.

The Grade II listed building is now a boutique hotel called Courthouse Hotel Shoreditch. Many of the period features of the Old Street Magistrates' Court have been retained and restored. The first of two courtrooms has been transformed into a casual fine dining restaurant, while the second is an exclusive members' only bar.

The courthouse cells where the Krays were held in 1965 for the business with Hew McCowan – have been converted into VIP booths. The 5ft x 15ft cells retain their metal reinforced doors and one cell still has its original hard bench and commode fitted. You can now hire out the cells – which are decorated in artwork of Ronnie and Reggie – to truly immerse yourself in the Old Street Magistrates' Court experience.

# Chapter 29

# The Old Bailey

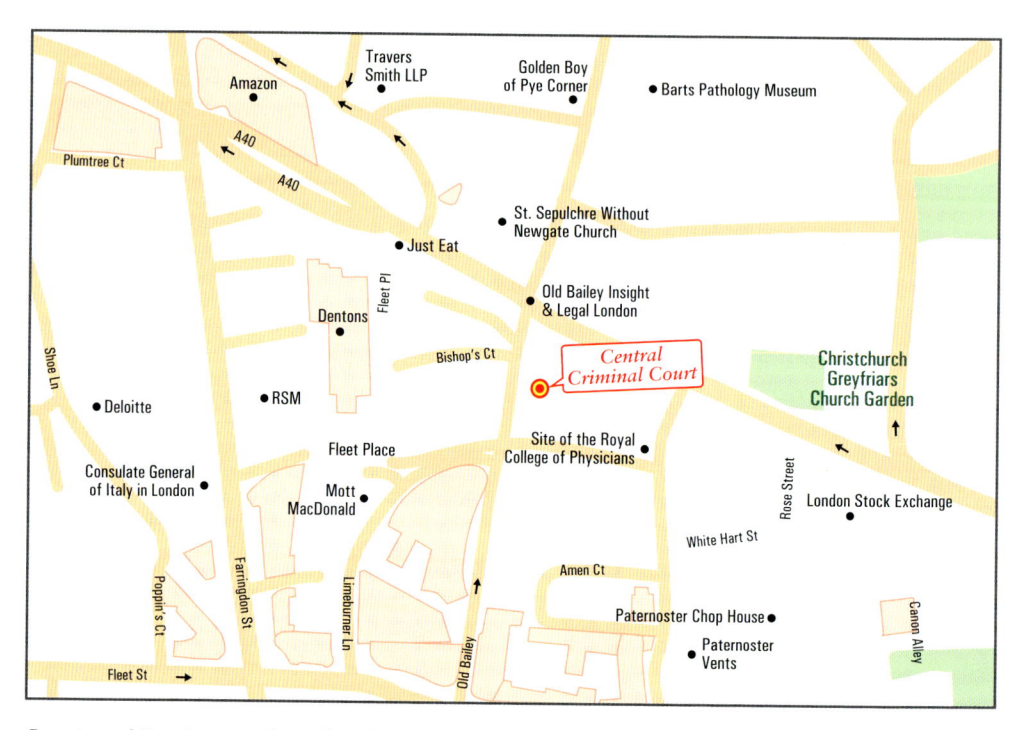

*Ronnie and Reggie were charged with the murders of Jack 'The Hat' McVitie and George Cornell at The Old Bailey.*

**Where?**
The Old Bailey
London
EC4M 7EH

**Why?**
Both Ronnie and Reggie were found guilty of murder here. It was one of the most highly publicised cases of its time.

## *The Old Bailey*

**How to get there:**
The Old Bailey is a quick walk from St Paul's Underground station. It takes seven minutes (0.3 miles) from the station. Once you've exited the station, walk left on Newgate Street passing the London Stock Exchange on your left. Continue walking until you reach Old Bailey situated on the left-hand side of the road. Walk down Old Bailey and the court can be found on the right.

The Old Bailey is the central criminal court of England and Wales. Famous in its own right, the court has been referred to for many centuries – it's believed the first mention of this iconic building was in 1585. It was completely destroyed in the Great Fire Of London in 1666 and rebuilt in 1674.

It's one of the most talked about courts in the UK and is featured countless times in books, TV programmes and the like, from *Pirates Of The Caribbean* to *A Tale Of Two Cities* by Charles Dickens. It also featured many high-profile cases, so Ronnie and Reggie's case was not out of the ordinary. Trials of the likes of Oscar Wilde and Peter Sutcliffe (The Yorkshire Ripper) were also conducted here.

It is important to note the significance of the Old Bailey; it's a building – and an area in London – which is used to regular high-profile cases. With this in mind, the Krays' case was one of the most high-profile cases the Old Bailey has ever seen. To highlight this, tickets for the public gallery were selling for £5 each on the black market – which is equivalent of almost £80 in today's money. Tickets to all court viewing areas are meant to be free.

It wasn't just Scotland Yard's case against the Kray twins that made history for being the most expensive of the time, the Old Bailey trial also broke records. It took thirty-nine days to convict the pair, which was the longest – and most expensive – case ever to be held at the Old Bailey.

The trial was held in Court number 1 and the police presence was palpable. They rushed around outside the court, busily talking into walkie talkies as each member of The Firm took to the dock to hear their verdicts.

Plain-clothed policemen kept 24-hour surveillance on the jury during the thirty-nine days of the trial. They followed each of them home each night and even let them into their houses to check there was nobody trying to influence them as they arrived home.

It wasn't just the jury and the defendants who were high-profile. There were many celebrities in the gallery including Charlton Heston; even Judy Garland sent the pair her well wishes via a telegram.

At 7.06 pm on 8 March 1969, the verdict was in. The jury took six hours and fifty-four minutes to come to a decision. The following verdicts were published in *The Guardian*:

The verdicts, all of which were unanimous, were in order of declaration:

Ronald Kray (34), of Bunhill Row, Islington, guilty of the murders of Jack 'The Hat' McVitie, a bookmaster's clerk, in a Hackney flat in

October 1967, and of the murder of George Cornell in the Blind Beggar public house, Whitechapel, in March 1966.

John Barrie (31), of no settled address, guilty of murdering Cornell.

Ronald's twin Reginald Kray, guilty of murdering McVitie and of being an accessory after the fact to Cornell's murder.

Christopher Lambrianou (29), of Queensbridge Road, Hackney, his brother Anthony Lambrianou (26), and Ronald Bender (30), of Cubitt Town, Poplar, guilty of murdering McVitie.

Anthony Barry (30), of Old Nazeing Road, Broxbourne, Hertfordshire, not guilty of murdering McVitie. He was discharged.

Charles Kray (42), of Rosefield Gardens, Tower Hamlets, Frederick Foreman (26), of Lant Street, Southwark, and Cornelius Whitehead (33), of Rosefield Gardens, guilty as accessories to McVitie's murder.

An eleventh man, Albert Donaghue (32), of Devons Road, Bow, had admitted this offence and will be sentenced today.

It is estimated that £150,000 was spent on the case at the Old Bailey. This includes the security and the legal costs. It's also suggested that a further £4,000 was spent on the jurors to cover their costs as well as employ 24-hour surveillance.

As each of the members of The Firm left the dock, only one – Christopher Lambrianou – showed any emotion; he was very upset by his verdict of guilty of murder.

The Old Bailey is famous for eliciting fear in even the most hardened of criminals. When the death penalty was still in operation, criminals would walk through a straight line of brick arches known as 'dead man's walk' after the judge had ordered their execution. The trip from the court to an open square outside of Newgate Prison – which used to sit next to the Old Bailey – would be the final trip the criminal would make.

At the end of the walk, the prisoner would turn left and into a place known as 'The Birdcage'. The Birdcage had a net covering it and it allowed natural light to seep in. This area was known as the last place the prisoners were able to see sunlight. In those days, prisoners would have a hood placed over their head before the hanging.

In the Krays' book, *Our Story*, Ronnie said that they would both have preferred to be hanged than spend their entire lives in prison. Thirty years each, in comparison to other similar cases, was a long sentence. The Prison Reform Trust's Una Padel said she believed the 'harsh' sentences for Ronnie and Reggie were as a direct result of the high emotion surrounding the case.

# Chapter 30

# All Saints Church

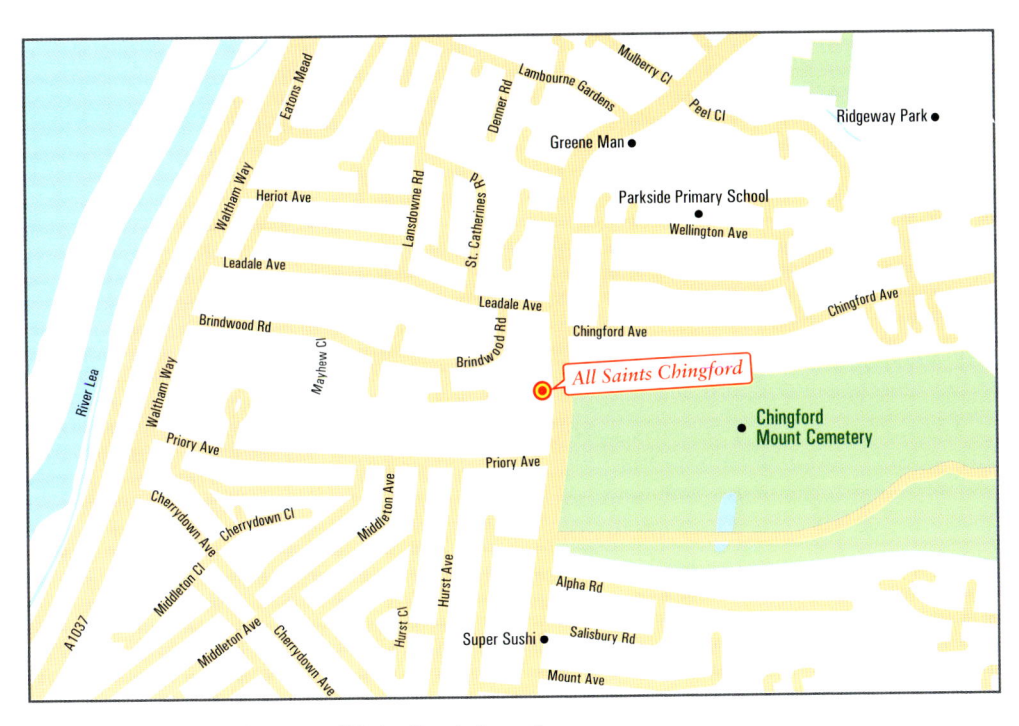

*All Saints Church, the location of Violet Kray's funeral.*

**Where?**
All Saints Church
184 Old Church Road
Chingford
London
E4 8BU

**Why?**
This is where Violet Kray's funeral took place in 1982. It's the first place Ronnie and Reggie were seen in over ten years after being let out on compassionate leave following Violet's death.

**How to get there:**
All Saints Church – and Chingford Mount where all the Kray family, including Ronnie and Reggie, are buried, is situated 1.5 miles (thirty-minute walk) from Chingford station. While it is possible to walk, many people choose to get a cab. It's quite a walk and it's recommended that you take a map with you.

This particular church is iconic because it's the location of the first time Ronnie and Reggie were seen in public after being imprisoned in 1969.

This was the church where Violet Kray's funeral took place on 11 August 1982. The widely attended service received some criticism from both Ronnie and Reggie. With the swarms of media and journalists camping outside, eagerly awaiting a glimpse of the duo. It was quite momentous that they were allowed out for their mother's funeral, but they were given special dispensation because of the relationship they had with her. She visited them every week at whatever prison they were in, in some cases travelling half way across the country.

They were almost mobbed going into the church and have both criticised the publicity around their mother's funeral. Ron said, 'It wasn't right. It wasn't fair. It should have been a private occasion.' He did, however, praise the police for perhaps one of the only times on record. He said they looked after them on the day of the funeral, giving them a cup of tea at Romford Police Station and allowing them to go to the funeral in the first place.

Everybody was in attendance, Charles and Charlie included. Charles died one year later. The twins didn't attend his funeral. He'd asked specifically for a quiet funeral and after the difficulties they found at Violet's funeral, everybody thought it best to keep it a low-key, private affair. His funeral took place at this church, too, and he was buried alongside Violet in the family plot.

All Saints Church, which is also called Chingford Old Church, was most probably chosen because of its proximity to Chingford Mount Cemetery – it's directly across the road. Violet was buried in the family's plot – along with Frances – in Chingford Mount Cemetery.

The church is a small, unassuming building. Its position opposite such a large, sprawling cemetery makes it look almost diminutive in comparison. It dates back to the twelfth century and is very in keeping with that period. From the stones used to build it to the shape of the windows, it has all the markings of a twelfth-century church, it also has a story of restoration, which is quite common of churches of the period.

In the 1840s it was lovingly known as the 'green church' because of the ivy that grew around it. It became rather famous in the 1840s as a place artists would come to recreate the beauty of the building. It soon became dilapidated, though, and had no use until its restoration in 1930. Nowadays, it's a very busy church and hall; it's in use most days for a range of activities from fitness classes to choir rehearsals.

# Chapter 31

# St Matthew's Church

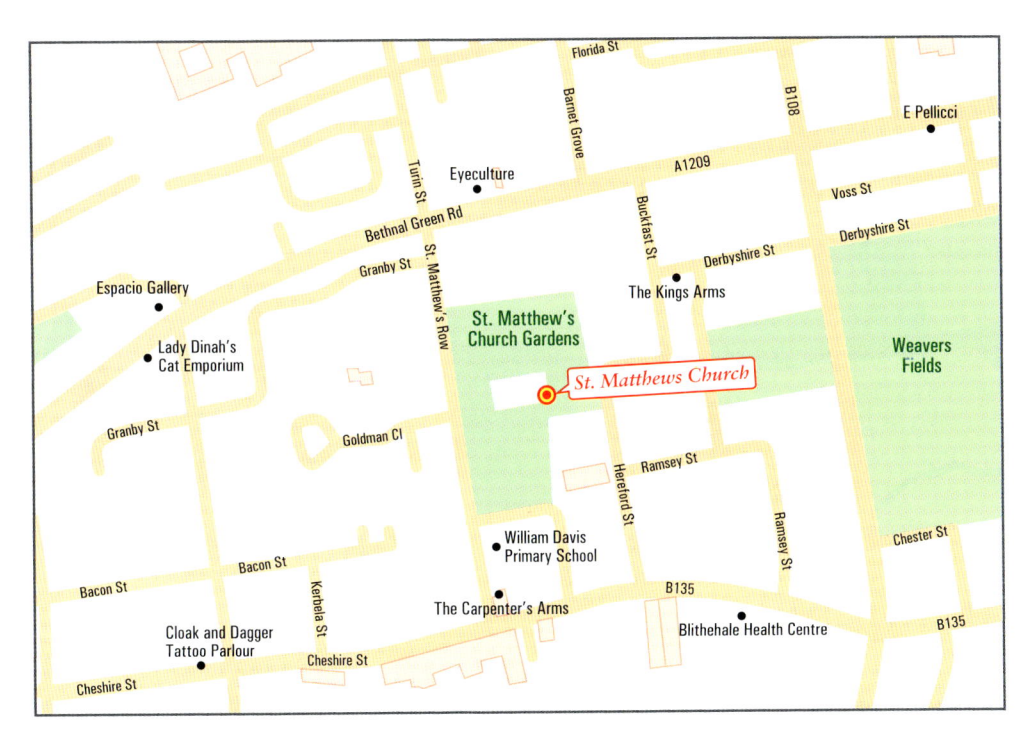

*St Matthew's Church; where both Ronnie and Reggie Kray's funerals were held.*

**Where?**
St Matthew's Church
St Matthew's Row
Bethnal Green
London
E2 6DT

**Why?**
Ronnie and Reggie's funerals took place here.

**How to get there:**
St Matthew's Church is situated a short walk from Repton Boxing Club, William Davis Primary School and The Carpenter's Arms. The Carpenter's Arms sits on the

corner of Cheshire Street and St Matthew's Row. Follow St Matthew's Row up until you see the church on the right.

This beautiful church, with sprawling gardens, can be found in St Matthew's Row, which is neatly wedged in between Cheshire Street and Bethnal Green Road. The church, which has similarities to St James The Great Church where Reggie and Frances got married, was the place where Ronnie, Reggie and Charlie's funerals were held.

Ronnie's funeral took place on 29 March 1995, Reggie's on 11 October 2000 and Charlie's on 19 April 2000. Each time, the church and the surrounding streets were full of thousands of mourners.

The church was rebuilt following the Second World War by Anthony Lewis of Michael, Tapper & Lewis. He then commissioned the sculptor Don Potter to create the church's Stations of the Cross. Much of the furniture and interiors of this church were surviving pieces from other bombed churches around London.

Anthony Lewis' vision was quite remarkable for his era; he commissioned a number of young artists to make key pieces for the church and then ensured they were integral to the structure of the building. Thus, moulding them into the foundations of the building forevermore.

Ronnie, who was still in Broadmoor, died of a heart attack aged 61 in Wexham Park Hospital, Slough, Berkshire. The magnitude of his funeral was beyond expectations; the police had to close large parts of the East End of London for the funeral procession to make its way through the streets. The pavements of each road it passed along were brimming with mourners.

*St Matthew's Church*

Reggie was permitted to attend the funeral and was greeted 'like a returning hero' according to a BBC News report from the day of Ronnie's funeral. It was the third time he had been allowed out of prison in twenty-seven years. There were queues of old friends leading to Reggie's pew in the church, all desperate to see their old friend.

Ronnie had a Victorian glass hearse covered in white flowers and drawn by six black horses. Reggie's wreath was displayed outside of the church and read 'to the other half of me'.

Charlie's funeral was next and took place just six months before Reggie's. He collapsed in Parkhurst Prison six months prior to his death and spent the remainder of his life in St Mary's Hospital, Newport on the Isle Of Wight. On the day of Charlie's death, which was recorded as from 'natural causes' on his death certificate, Reggie was released from prison to visit him. It wasn't the first visit. At this point, Reggie had served more than his recommended time in prison and was able to make repeated visits to see Charlie in the final months of his life. Charlie was buried in the family plot in Chingford Mount cemetery alongside Violet, Charles Senior, Ronnie and Frances.

Later that year, Reggie died after a battle with bladder cancer. The cancer was inoperable, and so he was released from prison under compassionate grounds to live his final days with his wife, Roberta.

## St Matthew's Church

Reggie met Roberta, who was twenty-five years his junior, when she was helping to publicise a film about Ronnie. They started talking over the phone and through letters and a year after they met, they were married in Maidstone Prison.

Similarly to Ronnie's funeral, Reggie's was a grand affair; the streets were lined with people. His procession toured around many of their old stomping grounds, including Cheshire Street past Repton Boxing Club and the Carpenter's Arms. As well as the large public and police presence, Reggie had a number of wreaths and flowers from celebrity friends, including Barbara Windsor.

As the procession wound through the streets, including Vallance Road, and made its way into St Matthew's Church the speakers belted the song *My Way* by Frank Sinatra. Not only was this particular song quite a poignant and fitting choice, Frank Sinatra was also a friend of Ronnie and Reggie's, giving it double meaning.

Reggie was the last of the Kray family to be buried at Chingford Cemetery alongside the rest of this family.

# Chapter 32

# W. English & Son

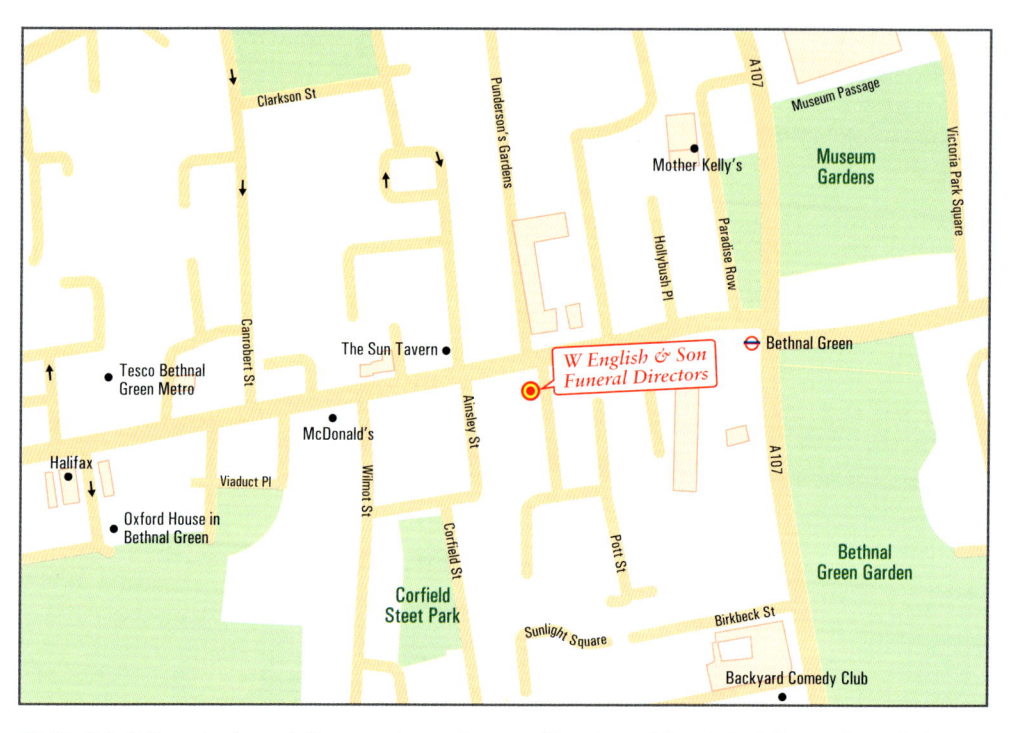

*W. English & Son; the funeral directors that took care of Ronnie and Reggie's elaborate funeral plans.*

**Where?**
W. English & Son
464a Bethnal Green Road
London
E2 0EA

**Why?**
W. English & Son is the undertakers that dealt with the funerals of Ronnie and Reggie Kray.

## *W. English & Son*

**How to get there:**
W. English & Son is the first stop of interest after getting off the tube at Bethnal Green Underground station. Head onto Bethnal Green Road and walk for about two minutes. You'll see W. English & Son's building on the left-hand side of the road on the corner of Pott Street.

Known as the 'undertakers of the underworld', W. English & Son funeral directors has become famous among East Enders. When asked which places reminded them of the Krays the most, a number of ex-Bethnal Green residents cited this funeral directors as a key place.

It was the company that handled the funerals of Ronnie, Reggie and Charlie.

For each funeral, a large number of people showed up outside W. English & Son and walked behind the hearse to St Matthew's Church – which is situated half a mile further along Bethnal Green Road, heading towards Shoreditch, on St Matthew's Row.

The funeral parlour specialises in both religious and non-religious funerals, but there was some controversy around the funeral chosen by Reggie Kray.

In the years leading to his death, it's reported that Reggie Kray had found God, but wasn't prepared to let anybody know about it, because he didn't want people to think his admission was simply a ploy to help him achieve parole.

Ken Stallard, an Evangelical Free Church Minister, delivered the funeral address and described himself as Reggie's spiritual advisor over the seventeen years before he died. Ken Stallard met Reggie through Ronnie. It has been reported that Ronnie also found God in prison.

At Reggie's funeral, Ken said:

> In both of these men were depths of spiritual feeling which the world never saw nor knew. So many people preferred to look at the bad rather than the good. Reg spent a great deal of money and a great deal of time looking after and caring for others.

The funeral directors is a short walk along Bethnal Green Road from Bethnal Green Underground station. As you walk along the road full of shops nestled underneath flats, W. English & Son is immediately apparent. The cream building, with its triangle roof has an aura about it; a look at years gone by.

There are some subtle differences between the building in its current state and the building that saw thousands of mourners gathered outside for Ronnie and Reggie's funerals. All of the differences, though, are aesthetic. The colour palette of the funeral parlour at the time of Reggie's funeral was white with green windows and green signage. Now, however, the signage has been replaced to facilitate the company's new colour palette: cream and maroon.

# Chapter 33

# Chingford Mount Cemetery

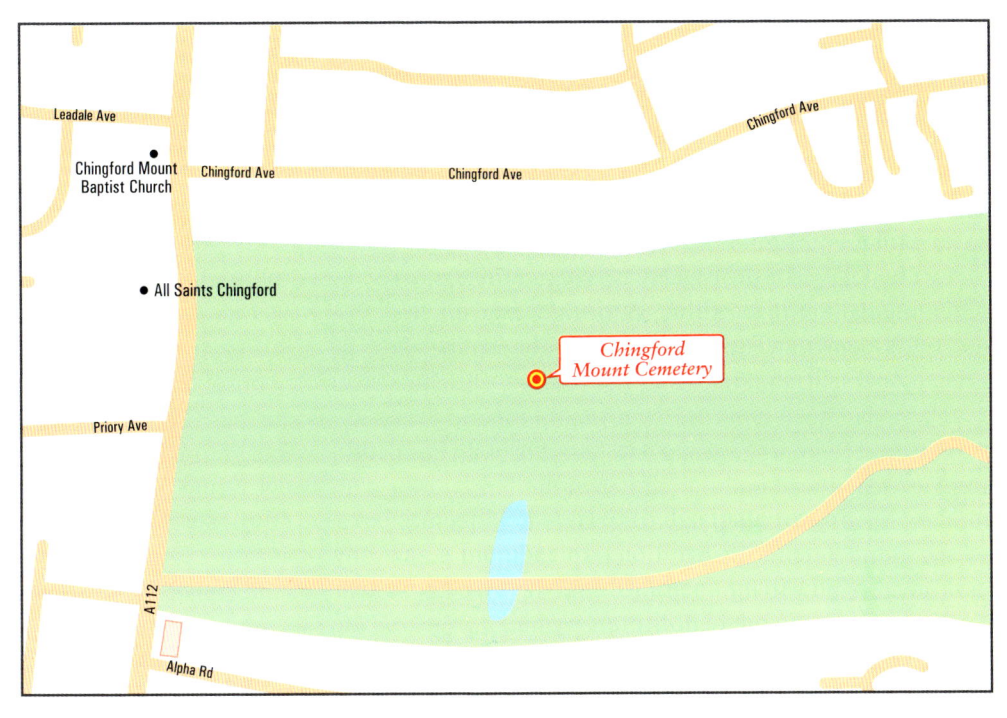

*Chingford Mount Cemetery, where all of the Kray family are buried.*

**Where?**
Chingford Mount Cemetery
121 Old Church Road
London
E4 6ST

**Why?**
Chingford Mount Cemetery is where all of the Krays, including Ronnie and Reggie, are buried.

**How to get there:**
Please follow the instructions set out under All Saints Church.

Chingford Mount Cemetery sits opposite All Saints Church and is the burial place for all of the Kray family. The plot covers 41.5 acres of land and was opened in May 1884 on the site of the house and grounds of Caroline Mount.

There were some doubts about the future of the unused parts of Chingford Mount Cemetery in the 1970s; the management company collapsed and there was talk of it being sold to create a housing development. The local residents halted the plans by filing their objections, and since then it has been in the care of London Borough of Waltham Forest council.

Most of the plots on this land are what would be described as 'war graves'. They belong to Commonwealth service personnel of both World Wars. Some of the graves have no headstones but there's a low screen wall featuring all of the names of the people buried there.

More recently, in 2016, Frances' grave was graffitied. It said 'remember Jack McVitie, George Cornell'. It was quickly professionally cleaned, but members of the Shea family were extremely unimpressed, saying that Frances had absolutely nothing to do with their murders.

Before Reggie was arrested, he visited Chingford Mount Cemetery to see Frances' grave regularly; sometimes several times in one day. When he was let out of prison on compassionate grounds six months before he died, he was photographed kissing Frances' grave at the funeral of his brother, Charlie.

There had been controversy around Frances' grave when she was first buried. Her parents told Reggie she wished to revert back to her maiden name before her death but Reggie went ahead and buried her in the family plot with her wedding dress on. Her mother, Elsie, persuaded the undertaker to put a slip on underneath her wedding dress so she didn't have to have it directly touching her skin.

You can find the family plot in the top left-hand corner of the cemetery. It's quite easy to miss, with the hundreds of surrounding graves, but the pictures on the front of Ronnie and Reggie's tombstone make it a little easier. Frances' grave is at the front and sits next to Violet and Charles; it's the largest of the tombstones.

# Sources

**Books**

Baker, T.F.T., *(ed.) A History Of The County Of Middlesex, Volume 11, Stepney, Bethnal Green*, 1998
Broad, Roger, *Conscription In Britain 1939–64*, Routledge, 2005
Fishman, William, *East End 1888*, Duckworth, 1998
Foreman, Freddie, *Respect*, Century, 1996
Hobbs, Richard, *Kray Brothers*, Oxford University Press, 2004
Kray, Charlie, *Doing The Business – The Final Confession of the Senior Kray Brother*, John Blake, 2011
Kray, Reggie and Gerrard, Peter, *Reggie Kray's East End Stories*, Sphere, 2010
Mayhew, Henry, *London Labour and The London Poor*, 1851
Morton, James, *Gangland Soho*, Little Brown, 1992
Palmer, Alan, *The East End,* John Murray, 1989
Pearson, John, *The Profession Of Violence,* Bloomsbury Reader, 1995
Read, Leonard, *The Man Who Nicked The Krays,* Time Warner Paperbacks, 2002
Teale, Bobby, *Bringing Down The Krays,* Ebury Press, 2012
Webb, Billy, *Running With The Krays: My Life In London's Gangland,* Mainstream Publishing, 1995
Windsor, Barbara, *All Of Me,* Headline Book Publishing, 2000
Wise, Sarah, *The Italian Boy: A Tale of Murder and Body Snatching in 1830s London*, Metropolitan Books, 2004

**Personal Interviews:**

King, Pat, Personal Interview. 12 Dec. 2017
Kyriacou, Chris, Personal Interview. 4 Apr. 2004
Lucas, Rosie, Personal Interview. 12 Dec. 2017

**Digital resources:**

Alexander, Ella, (14 May 2014) *Reggie Kray's Wife Frances Shea's Diaries,* Retrieved from: https://www.independent.co.uk/news/people/reggie-kray-s-wife-frances-shea-s-diaries-revealed-the-drunken-abuse-bedside-knives-and-constant-9369440.html

Brooke, Mike *Kray, twins got thick ear from Granny Kelly's east end pie 'n' mash owner* Retrieved from: http://www.eastlondonadvertiser.co.uk/news/heritage/kray-twins-got-thick-ear-from-granny-kelly-s-east-end-pie-n-mash-owner-1-3985764

Brooke, Mike *Vandals daub east London grave of gangster Reggie Kray's wife Frances* Retrieved from: http://www.eastlondonadvertiser.co.uk/news/vandals-daub-east-london-grave-of-gangster-reggie-kray-s-wife-frances-1-4729894

Browning, Richard, *Historic Inflation Calculator,* Retrieved from http://www.thisismoney.co.uk/money/bills/article-1633409/Historic-inflation-calculator-value-money-changed-1900.html

*Brixton Prison Information,* Retrieved from: http://www.justice.gov.uk/contacts/prison-finder/brixton

Chancellor, Alexander, *It's time to explode the myth that all children evacuated from the Blitz were well treated* Retrieved from: https://www.theguardian.com/commentisfree/2009/sep/03/alexander-chancellor-wartime-evacuees

*Chingford Mount Cemetery* Retrieved from: https://www.cwgc.org/find-a-cemetery/cemetery/38422/CHINGFORD%20MOUNT%20CEMETERY

Fountain, Daniel, *Former Old Street Magistrates' Court Becomes Boutique Hotel,* Retrieved from: https://hoteldesigns.net/industry-news/former-old-street-magistrates-court-becomes-boutique-hotel/

Ezard, John, *Krays will be sentenced for murder today,* Retrieved from: https://www.theguardian.com/uk/1969/mar/05/ukcrime.johnezard

*Gangland villain who mixed it with the Krays* Retrieved from: http://www.heraldscotland.com/news/12111031.Gangland_villain_who_mixed_it_with_the_Krays/

*G. Kelly History* Retrieved from: http://gkelly.london/history/

Girvan, Dan, *8 pubs with a seriously creepy history* Retrieved from: http://www.hammerfilms.com/8-watering-holes-seriously-creepy-history/

Hiscock, John, (24 February 2009) *The Real Casino Royale: Gangsters In A Class Of Their Own,* Retrieved from: http://www.telegraph.co.uk/culture/film/4735580/The-Real-Casino-Royale-gangsters-in-a-class-of-their-own.html

Horton, Tom, *Braithwaite House tenants 'told Islington Council about fire five years ago – but nothing was done',* Retrieved from: http://www.islingtongazette.co.uk/news/braithwaite-house-tenants-told-islington-council-about-fire-risk-years-ago-but-nothing-was-done-1-5082532

Jeffries, Stuart, (7 November 2001) *Carry On Up The East End,* Retrieved from: https://www.theguardian.com/film/2001/dec/07/artsfeatures

Oakley, Malcolm, (7 October 2013), *World War Two And East London,* Retrieved from: http://www.eastlondonhistory.co.uk/world-war-2-east-london/

O'Niell, Sean *East End Says Goodbye To The Last Of The Krays* Retrieved from: https://www.telegraph.co.uk/news/uknews/1370000/East-End-says-farewell-to-last-of-the-Krays.html

*Oxford House* Retrieved from: https://www.oxfordhouse.org.uk/about/introduction/ and https://www.oxfordhouse.org.uk/repton-boxing/

*Royal Borough Of Kensington & Chelsea, Virtual Museum, List Of Famous Residents,* Retrieved from: https://www.rbkc.gov.uk/vmpeople/infamous/peterrachman.asp

*Sources*

*Survey Of London,* Retrieved from: *https://surveyoflondon.org/map/feature/496/detail/*
*The Evacuated Children Of The Second World War* Retrieved from *https://www.iwm.org.uk/history/the-evacuated-children-of-the-second-world-war*
The Idle Man, *How To Dress Like The Kray Twins,* Retrieved from: *https://theidleman.com/manual/advice/how-dress-kray-twins/*